INVASION OF PRIVACY

INVASION OF PRIVACY

How to Protect Yourself in the Digital Age

Michael S. Hyatt

Since 1947
**REGNERY
PUBLISHING, INC.**
An Eagle Publishing Company • Washington, DC

Cataloging-in-Publication Data on file with the Library of Congress

Published in the United States by
Regnery Publishing, Inc.
An Eagle Publishing Company
One Massachusetts Avenue, NW
Washington, DC 20001

Visit us at www.regnery.com

Distributed to the trade by
National Book Network
4720-A Boston Way
Lanham, MD 20706

Printed on acid-free paper
Manufactured in the United States of America

10 9 8 7 6 5 4 3 2 1

BOOK DESIGN BY KASHKA KISZTELINSKA
SET IN JANSON

Books are available in quantity for promotional or premium use. Write to Director of Special Sales, Regnery Publishing, Inc., One Massachusetts Avenue, NW, Washington, DC 20001, for information on discounts and terms or call (202) 216–0600.

The author is engaged in providing certain information that he believes, at the time of writing, to be an accurate representation of the facts. However, this publication is for informational purposes only. It is not intended to provide legal, accounting, or tax advice. Persons needing such advice are encouraged to seek private and professional counsel. All information should be used as a general guide only and not as the ultimate source of information. Neither the author nor the publisher shall have any liability or responsibility to any person or entity with respect to any loss or damage caused, or alleged to be caused, directly or indirectly, by any information provided.

Every good faith effort has been made in this work to credit sources and comply with the fairness doctrine on quotation and use of research material. If any copyrighted material has been inadvertently used in this work without proper credit being given in one manner or another, please notify the publisher in writing so that future printings of this work may be corrected accordingly.

To my dad, who rightly taught me that
some things are no one else's business

If you are interested in having Michael Hyatt
speak to your group, please contact:

Institute for Personal Privacy
4683 Trousdale Drive
Nashville, TN 37024
(615) 371-1378

CONTENTS

PRACTICAL PRIVACY TIPS

THE END OF PRIVACY?

Modern Americans are so exposed, peered at, inquired about, and spied upon as to be increasingly without privacy—members of a naked society and denizens of a goldfish bowl.
—Senator Edward V. Long

I was about twelve. I had just returned home from a sleepover at my buddy's house. "Dad," I began naively, "Jeff says his dad makes more than fifty thousand bucks a year. How much do you make?"

I'll never forget my dad's response. It was short and to the point. "Son, that's none of your business." I felt a flush of embarrassment, knowing that I had just crossed an invisible line.

Although I didn't know it at the time, that brief encounter was my first and best lesson on privacy. I learned that some things were *public* and some were *private*. A high wall of civility and social convention separated the two. Only the ignorant or ill mannered would attempt to scale that tall and prickly barrier.

I never did learn how much my dad made, and, quite frankly, after that day I didn't want to know. I assumed that this was just the way the world was—some things were meant to be private.

My, how times have changed!

OUR PRESENT CRISIS

Americans—and indeed people across the developed world— are in the midst of a crisis. You may not realize there is a crisis, but this only makes the situation that much more dangerous. Right now, whether you realize it or not, you are exposed and vulnerable.

The crisis is quite simple: privacy is ending. Your home address and phone number, your Social Security number, your bank accounts, your credit history, your shopping habits, your work history, your travel habits—all are readily available to anyone who might be interested in them. Thanks to technological developments in computing and telecommunications—the two fundamental pillars of the Internet—information that was once relatively innocuous because it was not collated with other databases can now be pulled together and accessed like never before. Worse, the government and various institutions have the means to collect far more data about you than they could previously.

But technology is only part of the problem. When, in the 1960s, Senator Edward V. Long lamented that Americans were "increasingly without privacy," the technological innovations that we now associate with the invasion of privacy were in many cases decades away. Yes, computers make it easier and more convenient to build comprehensive profiles about individual citizens. Yes, the Internet has given all of us near-instant access to information that used to take days, if not weeks, for professional investigators to assemble. But ultimately privacy is at stake because of how we have reacted to these technological developments, how we've shifted away from expecting privacy. As you will see, in many ways we have become the problem. Because people have the *ability* to know the intimate details of other people's lives, they have begun to think they have the *right* to know. This new cultural phenomenon has created many new risks for those who value their privacy.

Marketing Manipulation

Most of your mail and many of your phone calls come from marketers who have evaluated your profile and decided that they can convince you to give them some money. Banks regularly sell comprehensive profiles to telemarketers, including detailed account information—spending patterns, payment histories, credit limits, and more. Salesmen aren't the only ones who use this information; charities, political groups, universities, and others get access to these profiles. Even medical records are bought and sold; though you might think you are covered by doctor-patient confidentiality, the ever present insurance companies make no such promises of privacy.

To see the ramifications of such marketing manipulation, consider the following true stories:

- Across the country, people began receiving a letter from Rite Aid Corporation. "The fact is," the letter said, "you could be one of the 17 million Americans whose age and high cholesterol puts them at risk of a first heart attack." But Rite Aid wasn't just looking out for the welfare of Americans: the letter was a sales pitch for a new cholesterol-lowering medicine. Rite Aid was using prescription lists to target those being treated for high cholesterol. Other pharmacies have done the same with their prescription lists, peddling allergy treatments, heart medication, treatments for venereal disease, stop-smoking medication, and much more.[1]

- Picking up her phone, a Canadian woman was taken aback when the caller asked for her by her first name. The woman's phone number was unlisted, and she didn't know the person on the other end of the line. It turns out the caller was a political pollster. How, the woman wondered, did pollsters get her name and phone number?[2] One possible explanation is that she had at some point called a toll-free number that had recorded her information. Most 800 numbers can identify the caller's phone number even if it's unlisted.[3]

- Like millions of other Americans, Beverly filled out a direct-mail product questionnaire in exchange for some coupons. But she ended up getting far more than product discounts. Several weeks later, she received a letter from a stranger who graphically described sexual acts he wanted to perform on her. The stranger knew many details about her: her birthday, what magazines she read, even what brand of soap she used. How did he know all this? He was a prison inmate who performed data entry for Metromail, the company that issued the product questionnaire Beverly had filled out. The prisoner used the information for his own purposes, obviously, but meanwhile, Metromail added her detailed profile to its massive database, which has information on more than 90 percent of America's households. The company regularly sells profiles from this database.[4]

Credit Card Fraud

This is a real problem that has only grown worse with the proliferation of credit cards. Recently, three ladies in my office had their purses stolen by a temp. Before they knew what had happened, the perpetrator had charged hundreds of dollars to their credit cards. After spending weeks trying to get the mess straightened out, they are, as I am writing this, still dealing with the aftermath. Other people in similar situations have spent *years* trying to get their credit history repaired. And just about anyone can be victimized:

- Ed never bought anything on the Internet, so he figured his credit cards were safe. He was wrong. A thief didn't need to intercept his number online; he just needed an old receipt. Soon, fraudulent charges began appearing on Ed's credit card bill. Many of them were for pornographic Web sites.[5]
- Audri and Jim publish an award-winning e-newsletter about Internet fraud. But their knowledge of the problem couldn't prevent them from falling victim to a credit card scam. Audri and Jim also run an online store, and the couple began to receive complaints from people who said they had been charged for products they had never ordered. As it happens, an employee at a sporting goods stores had taken customers' names and credit card numbers and opened e-mail accounts under these names. The employee was thus able to circumvent normal credit card security checks and use the stolen card numbers to order merchandise from Audri and Jim's site.[6]

Identity Theft

Though you may think this is unlikely to affect you, identity theft is a mushrooming problem. And the problem goes far beyond ruined credit. Identity thieves, who need only a Social Security number to operate, have been known to commit other crimes while using someone else's identity. As a result, the victim of identity theft himself becomes a suspect. Even identity thieves who look nothing like their victims have managed to cast suspicion on them by committing crimes using their names. Often the victim's attempts to explain the situation to creditors and police officials are met with hostility and suspicion. If you are a victim, you may have to pay exorbitant lawyer's fees to defend yourself against crimes you never committed. Worse, identity thieves have been known to share numbers so that the same person is victimized again and again.

Here are just a few real-life examples of identity theft:

- Tiger Woods is a victim of identity theft. Yes, the number one golfer in the world—one of the most recognizable people in America—had his identity stolen. In December 2000, Woods told a jury how a California man had used his Social Security number to get a driver's license and credit cards under his real name, Eldrick T. Woods. Authorities accused the man of charging more than $17,000 to cards in the golfer's name.[7]

- Maureen and Ray were always careful to protect their privacy. They made sure they checked their credit reports, they never used the Internet for shopping or banking, and they hardly ever ordered from catalogs. But it still wasn't enough. Someone got Ray's Social Security number and used it to rack up more than $100,000 in debt—getting credit cards, buying two cars, and even securing a personal loan in Ray's name.[8]

- Norma was shocked when the insurance company notified her that it was raising her rates. The company attributed the increase to her recent conviction for drunk driving. But Norma doesn't drink. Another woman had stolen her identity and been committing crimes in her name. Norma told authorities, "She could still be out there doing the same thing, and I could get pulled over and go to jail."[9]

Stalking

This crime is also on the rise. It is particularly frightening because it can involve not only harassment but also violence and ultimately even death. Advances in technology have enabled stalkers to track their victims efficiently. A stalker no longer has to follow you in order to find out where you live. With a few dollars he can find out all about you via an Internet private investigation service. So even moving won't be much of a deterrent. Within a few days, a determined stalker can discover your new address and where you work.

This example offers some perspective on how stalkers work:

- Thomas was a husband and father. He was also a stalker. Though he would trail women to find out where they lived or worked, he didn't rely on that entirely. Thomas had ways to find out their names, addresses, and Social Security numbers. Often he would stand behind women in line at the supermarket and memorize the information on their checks, and he also had access to a pediatrician's office, where he would look up the names and Social Security numbers of patients' mothers. When he was finally arrested, he confessed to stalking thousands of women and raping two.[10]

Frozen Assets

Through the Financial Crimes Enforcement Network (FinCEN), the U.S. government and its allies are monitoring day-to-day financial transactions. This surveillance would be bad enough if the government were simply looking for bona fide criminal activity. But that's not the case. Officials are looking for suspicious behavior that might *appear* to warrant an investigation. And, oh, by the way, while they are conducting the investigation, they might just decide to freeze your accounts without charging you with a crime. It's happening every day.

Frivolous Lawsuits

Sadly, our present legal system can be used as a tool to plunder other people. The end of privacy means that nearly anyone with a little know-how and determination can get a list of your assets to decide if you are worth suing. If you own any significant property (real estate, brokerage accounts, retirement accounts, royalty income, and so forth), you could find yourself involved in a frivolous—and costly—lawsuit.

Employment Insecurity

Should a prospective employer be able to examine your college driving record when the job has nothing to do with your driving? Employers regularly gain access to all sorts of information about their prospective employees—information that is arguably none of their business—and discriminate accordingly. This is often done without the prospective employee's knowledge. In fact, entire companies specialize in providing this information for a modest fee. And more and more companies are surreptitiously monitoring employee communications, including e-mail, voice mail, and live phone conversations.

Often it seems as if employers believe there is no privacy in the workplace. Thus we see developments like the following:

- In June 2000, the online delivery company Kozmo.com fired a dozen employees who refused to submit to company background checks—investigations that would have looked at credit histories, driving records, potential criminal backgrounds, even "modes of living." After public outcry, Kozmo revised the consent form all employees were required to sign, narrowing the scope of the background checks. The company also offered to rehire the employees who had been fired—if they passed a criminal background check.[11]

Government Surveillance

The government is increasingly tracking the movements of innocent citizens and doing so as a matter of policy, not as the result of a warrant and reasonable suspicion. Any opposition to this trend is greeted by the response that if a person is not doing anything wrong, he should have nothing to hide. Through the intelligence network and monitoring system known as Echelon, authorities monitor virtually every transmission of any kind for keywords that might warrant further investigation. Moreover, the FBI is pushing the use of Carnivore, a program that intercepts and monitors e-mail without any external control over what law enforcement agencies see. Internet service providers are expected simply to allow a government agency to hook up a black box to their system and trust the agents to look at only those e-mails that a court order has given them permission to intercept.

Take the following, a case in which privacy was again trampled, theoretically in the interests of security:

- Excited fans poured into the stadium for Super Bowl XXV. But most had no idea that government officials were watching them. Law enforcement video cameras captured the face of every person who walked through the turnstiles. Each image was quickly digitized and checked against law enforcement records of known criminals—files from local and state police, the FBI, and other agencies. Privacy advocates objected that such measures amount to a "Big Brother"–type intrusion. Of course, officials justify these surveillance systems by saying they protect the safety of the people.[12]

GETTING PERSONAL

I didn't think about privacy much until it began to affect me personally. Because of the lesson I learned from my dad, I assumed that everyone operated on pretty much the same set of assumptions. Boy, was I wrong!

After the publication of my first book, I appeared on hundreds of radio and television shows. It didn't take long before my own privacy began to disappear.

First, I began to get unsolicited calls from the media. When this became annoying, we changed our phone number to an unlisted one. Unfortunately, this didn't seem to help. Soon I was getting calls not only from the media but also from readers seeking personal advice. I tried to be polite, but ultimately we had to disconnect that number and get an entirely new one. Even then, people would show up uninvited at the front door, asking if they could see me.

E-mail was even worse. For a while, I was getting a hundred or more e-mail messages a day from people I didn't know. Some messages were insulting and rude; a couple were downright threatening. I grew concerned about my family's safety. As a result, we went to considerable lengths to protect ourselves.

An eye-opening experience in the fall of 1998 made me realize that a few individuals weren't the only threat to my privacy. At that time I was asked to testify before Congress on the possible effects of Y2K on consumers. After my testimony I met with congressional committee staffers who were on loan from the alphabet soup agencies—the CIA, NSA, FBI, and so on.

In talking to one of the senior staffers I began to explain my work, but he stopped me short. "No need to explain," he stated matter-of-factly. "We know all about you." He then pulled out a thick stack of files with my name on them.

"We have a copy of everything you have ever written and a couple of your speeches too. We know just about everything there is to know." To me, it was frightening that everything I was doing was under this kind of scrutiny.

Perhaps you are thinking, *That's interesting, but it will never happen to me. I'm just an ordinary Joe (or Joanna).* I wish it were that simple.

The truth is that people know more about you than you could ever imagine. My situation is graphic but not atypical. The key is that anyone with a little ingenuity—or a pretext—can get your phone number and address, Social Security number and credit history, bank account records and credit card transactions, driving history, medical records, and more and begin to build a comprehensive profile. State-of-the-art database storage and retrieval systems have made this possible as never before. Marketers do it all the time. Criminals and lawyers are doing it with greater and greater frequency. Even the government is doing it, looking for patterns of suspicious behavior. It's not just my privacy that came to an end; yours is in jeopardy too.

ANOTHER KIND OF BOOK

Most privacy books fall into one of two categories. First, the best-known books focus almost exclusively on the problem. They detail one horror story after another and explain how technology is making privacy nearly impossible. These books may scare you, but they offer precious little in the way of practical guidance.

The second category focuses on solutions, all right, but these books seem to be written for people with something to hide—those in trouble with the law or the IRS, ex-spouses seeking to shirk their responsibilities, or those trying to scam others and protect their identity in the process.

This book is different. It will explain the problem because awareness is the first step in reclaiming your privacy, but it won't stop there. It will help you determine an appropriate level of privacy based on your lifestyle, financial resources, and personal values. One of my goals with this book is to provide you with reasonable privacy initiatives, so I have offered specific, real-world countermeasures that I have personally employed in my own quest for privacy, as have many others in theirs.

Let me warn you: this book will take you out of your comfort zone. You will learn about threats and risks you may have never considered before. But better to learn about the invasion of privacy from a book than by discovering that bank accounts have been opened in your name or by having your assets frozen because you withdrew more cash than usual from the bank. To be forewarned is to be forearmed.

HOW TO READ THIS BOOK

I suggest that you start by reading Appendix A: A Privacy Self-Assessment. This will help you determine where you are now in terms of privacy. You may be surprised at the results. Most people don't realize how vulnerable they truly are. But even if you are vulnerable, you will quickly learn how to protect yourself and those you care about.

The first part of the book focuses on the threats to our privacy: corporations, criminals, and the government itself. It will help you see why and how they are destroying your privacy. It's my hope that these four chapters will provide you with the motivation to reclaim your privacy.

The second part will help you decide what you want to do about these threats. I don't presume that everyone has the same needs or commitment to privacy. This section will help you determine a level of privacy appropriate to your objectives and lifestyle considerations.

The third part is dedicated to providing specific countermeasures: the nuts and bolts of reclaiming—and then maintaining—your personal privacy.[13]

Be advised that the quest for privacy is an ongoing one. Some strategies that work now may not work a few months or years from now. That's why I have set up a Web site to keep you on the cutting edge of privacy technology. You can find it at www.moreprivacy.com.

CONCLUSION

My hopes for this book are twofold. First and foremost I hope it will inspire you to protect yourself by taking steps to reclaim and preserve your privacy. Second, I hope that it will do the same for enough people that we start seeing a shift in present trends that are bringing privacy to an end. I would like our children and our children's children to live in a world where their privacy is protected. That will not happen unless you and I take concrete action now, while there is still time.

I really believe that we are at the "tipping point": the future of privacy—and perhaps freedom itself—will be decided in our lifetimes. Whether we lose it entirely or win it back depends in large part on what you do to reclaim your own privacy.

Let's begin.

PART ONE

UNDERSTAND THE THREAT

CHAPTER ONE

THE BEAST COMETH

No more secrets.

—Company motto for Docusearch, Inc.

Amy Boyer was being tracked. The beautiful young girl was soon to graduate from college. Not yet twenty-one, Amy was still living at home with her family, whom she loved greatly. She and her boyfriend were planning to purchase a home and begin the next stage of their life together. A hard worker, she held two part-time jobs while she attended school. With many friends and a loving family, she had no reason to think she had any enemies.[1]

Liam Youens was a young man who had gone to school with Amy. From at least the tenth grade he had been obsessed with her. Eventually he began a Web page to chronicle the ways in which he watched her. He discussed how he planned to kill her, her family, and then himself. But he had difficulty keeping tabs on Amy. He had dropped out of college after a year and was living at home, which afforded him limited use of a car. Amy often wasn't home when he was driving by to spy on her—she was probably working—and Youens needed to find out where she was if he was going to carry out his plan.

He was able to find Amy because she was being tracked—just as we all are. Youens simply needed to know who could pull together the information available in public documents and elsewhere. Using the Internet, he paid for several public record searches for personal information about Amy. He then obtained her Social Security number from Docusearch.com, a private investigation agency in Boca Raton, Florida. Finally, he paid $109 to get the address of Amy's workplace.

At 4:30 P.M. on October 15, 1999, Amy left her job at a dental office. As she was getting into her car, Youens pulled up, jumped from his vehicle, and fired fifteen shots into her. Her injuries included a fatal head wound. Youens used the sixteenth bullet to shoot himself in the head.[2]

WELCOME TO THE PANOPTICON

Amy Boyer was unique in many ways, but her vulnerability was anything but atypical. There was nothing about her that made her especially easy to track. She had a Social Security number, just like you do. She lived in a society in which private investigation firms advertise over the Internet and perform investigations for customers they never meet, just like you do. Her place of employment and other details of her life were available to anyone who wanted to spend a few dollars, and the same is undoubtedly true of you. Amy was a victim precisely because it has become relatively cheap and easy for *anyone* to get the information necessary to track a person down. Her stalker found out everything he needed to know without her ever knowing she was the object of his study.

Amy's tragic death has spurred some late, but important, discussion of the need for privacy in modern life. There has even been a bill proposed that would forbid companies from refusing services to someone who will not reveal his Social Security number. Another proposed bill would, as *New York Times* columnist William Safire points out, "[prohibit] individuals from 'displaying to the public' anybody's Social Security number without consent."[3] But even that legislation would exempt the "information brokers" that gave Liam Youens the information he needed to find and kill Amy Boyer.

Although such efforts to protect privacy are a start, in truth they do not take into account the deep-rooted nature of the problem. For instance, even while the use of Social Security numbers has proved so dangerous, many states still prominently display them on their driver's licenses. We are coming closer and closer to living in the "panopticon"—a world of total surveillance.

In 1787 Jeremy Bentham, a British philosopher, made a proposal for prison architecture called a "panopticon" (literally, "the all-seeing thing"). The idea behind the panopticon was that a prison would be most secure when the jailors watched the prisoners at all times. Since that was not possible, the next best solution was a structure where the guards *could* watch the prisoners at all times and where the prisoners never knew *if* they were being watched. That way, the prisoners would always behave appropriately.

Bentham never sold the British government on his plan, but he has proven to be something of a visionary nonetheless. Our society has become a sort of panopticon. It is all too easy to monitor someone without his knowing about it. We never know when the civil government, corporations, or predators are watching us. Unlike Bentham's prison, which had only one set of watchers, we are now in a situation in which any number of people might be watching us in different ways and at different times. We are being tracked, or at least we can never know for sure that we're *not* being tracked.

WHAT WILL IT TAKE?

As tragic as Amy Boyer's death is, it probably won't be enough to galvanize the public. Why? Because even though stalking is a growing problem in our society, being killed by a troubled youth—certainly a terrifying possibility—is still not all that likely. The fact is, however, that there are many other ways in which we can be victims of the panopticon. Indeed, even after her death, Amy was a victim of yet another invasion of privacy. The August before she died, Amy's pocketbook had been stolen, so she cancelled her credit cards and checks, thinking that was the end of it. But two days after her death made the news in New England, the thieves, who had gotten her Social Security number, were able to assume her identity. They managed to spend $5,000 by using checks in her name.[4]

Whether you realize it or not, you are being tracked, just as Amy Boyer was, and it can cost you time, money, and freedom. You are being tracked by just about anyone who thinks he can sell to you, steal from you, or control you. This includes government agencies and big businesses; banks, credit reporting agencies, and other financial information resellers; insurance companies, pharmacies, and other health-related organizations; political and extremist groups; local retail outlets and marketers; employers and fellow employees; spouses, ex-spouses, and potential spouses; lawyers and private investigators; and even common criminals, hackers, and practical jokers.

This is not merely an Internet problem. It is true that technological progress in data storage and data transfer has made it possible for others to monitor you more easily and to gather your personal information more speedily. It is also true that communication over the Internet has brought about new ways in which you can be scrutinized. These problems are real, and I will devote many pages to computer and Internet privacy in the chapters ahead. Nevertheless, the issue is not the Internet per se. Even if you don't use a computer, your activity is still being tracked, and your identity is vulnerable to those who wish to learn about you for whatever reason. In 1989, long before the Internet was a reality, a stalker was able to find and kill *My Sister Sam* sitcom star Rebecca Schaeffer by using motor-vehicle registration records in California.

Advances in technology are only making the problem worse. We are being tracked with increasing efficiency. We are being tracked more affordably. And we are being tracked more uniformly as various institutions share information with one another.

WHO IS TAKING AWAY OUR PRIVACY?

Many different groups offer rationales for why we need to expect all our personal information to be available to whoever wants it. The two main legitimate proponents of the panopticon are business interests and various government agencies. But professional criminals also benefit from this situation. I will devote a chapter to each in the pages ahead, but I want to provide an overview here.

Within the Law: The Corporate Perspective

Businesses obviously want to gain new customers and keep the customers they have. To do this, they need information. It is the fuel that drives modern industry. The more information a business has about a prospect or a customer, the more likely it can meet that customer's needs or shape its promotions to appeal to those needs. The information about a customer is called a "profile." It contains both demographic and psychographic data—not only who the person is but also what he does and why he does it. As a business collects more and more data about its customers, it soon discovers that such data are an asset that can be sold on the open market.

Businesses now routinely sell customer profiles to anyone who will pay for them. This has become a big problem in some industries, such as financial services. As a result of deregulation, one company can offer a full range of financial services: banking, insurance, investment brokerage, and direct marketing. Thus, the lure of "one-stop shopping" allows a single company to know a customer's *entire* financial situation.

This information can be, and sometimes is, used to exploit the customer. For example, U.S. Bancorp in Minnesota sold the personal account information of its customers to a telemarketing company for over $4 million plus a 22 percent commission on whatever sales were generated from the database.[5] As the Minnesota attorney general's office reported:

> [U.S. Bancorp] provided MemberWorks Inc. with the following information for its customers: name, address, telephone numbers of the primary and secondary customer, gender, marital status, homeownership status, occupation, checking account number, credit card number, Social Security number, birth date, account open date, average account balance, account frequency information, credit limit, credit insurance status, year to date finance charges, automated transactions authorized, credit card type and brand, number of credit cards, cash advance amount, behavior score, bankruptcy score, date of last payment, amount of last payment, date of last statement, and statement balance.[6]

Above the Law: The Government's Perspective

In our society, government is responsible for punishing criminals, protecting citizens, and preventing crimes—and for any number of other services. The government has used this as a rationale for all sorts of information gathering and surveillance. We are constantly being tracked by Big Brother through a variety of means—birth certificates, tax forms, motor vehicle registration, marriage certificates, voter registration, property records, court records, arrest records, divorce records, death certificates, and on and on.

Even where the government is entrusted to protect privacy, it does not reliably do so. Laws protecting privacy are helpful only if they are obeyed and enforced. For instance, an Ohio public school sold information to a bank about some of its students, enabling the bank to solicit business from the parents—despite the fact that it is illegal for public schools to provide such information to anyone without the parents' consent.[7]

Casual record keeping and failure to comply with the law are just part of the problem. Various government projects systematically invade our privacy. The National Security Agency (NSA), for example, has developed Echelon, a comprehensive spy network that monitors communication around the world. The Treasury Department has formed FinCEN, a network for retrieving personal financial information in real time. The FBI is now deploying Carnivore, a program that intercepts and reads e-mail on a mass scale.

Of course, many would not argue with the government's desire to protect us by stopping violent crime before it happens or to prevent money laundering, drug trafficking, tax evasion, and so on. But what happens when government agencies invade our individual rights? As we will see when we examine these new networks and technologies in greater detail, we are losing our privacy to the government, and in the process we are falling under its control.

More and more we find that we must simply depend on unaccountable government agencies not to violate our rights.

Outside the Law: The Criminal Perspective

The government and even some private industries consider access to our personal information an important way to prevent, detect, and solve crimes. But even if that were true, a concern is that the information superhighway is not restricted to authorized drivers. Criminals can, and do, use the panopticon to gain the information and control necessary to exploit others. In other words, the very means that the government and businesses employ for security purposes can actually lead to crime.

Perhaps the most egregious example of this sort of "safety equals vulnerability" equation is the ubiquitous Social Security number and its use in stalking and identity theft. As we saw with Amy Boyer, the Social Security number is a magic key that gives stalkers access to almost any other information they wish to have. (The other key is the target's name plus date of birth.) The Social Security number—which predators can get through theft, fraud, or hacking—also allows identity thieves to impersonate their victims, putting them into debt and committing other crimes under their names. The information superhighway, so efficient at spreading information, ruins the reputation of victims of identity theft; reports are spread to credit and law enforcement agencies of debts the victims never incurred and crimes they never committed. Victims report that both police and credit officials often treat them as perpetrators.

Consider what Kimo, a thirty-six-year-old programming consultant, had to go through after his identity was stolen. As the *San Francisco Chronicle* reported, someone got access to Kimo's Social Security number and driver's license number and was able to get credit cards in Kimo's name. In a matter of four months, the thief managed to charge more than $10,000. Because the charges were fraudulent, Kimo technically wasn't responsible for paying off this massive debt, but that didn't mean his worries were over. In just the first month after he discovered he was a victim of identity theft, Kimo spent fifty hours working to cancel accounts, straighten out his credit record, and deal with the police and the government. And that was just the beginning.

The *Chronicle* did an excellent job of reporting the numerous obstacles Kimo faced as he fought to clear his name and find out who the thief was. One of the biggest problems he encountered was that few were willing or able to help. For instance, although state law guaranteed that he could file a report with the police, he found that the local police department couldn't follow up on the case because it lacked manpower. Moreover, when Kimo first learned of the identity theft, he asked a bank that had issued a fraudulent card to give him the address that the thief had used; the bank refused. Another bank initially wouldn't consider some charges fraudulent. It seems the thief not only had gotten new cards in Kimo's name but also had charged items to his victim's existing card numbers, so Kimo had to provide proof that the charges were not his own. Similarly, Kimo's attempts to get a new driver's license number from the Department of Motor Vehicles were frustrating, as he had to battle through the bureaucracy and provide a slew of paperwork proving that he was a victim of identity theft.[8]

Kimo's case is instructive in another sense: before this happened to him, he had considered himself a "privacy freak." He always shredded his mail and regularly monitored his credit report. It didn't matter. The thief got his information off a rental application he had had to fill out when looking for an apartment.[9] Identity theft can happen to anyone.

And lest you think that Kimo's is an isolated case, be aware that identity theft is an increasingly common crime, one that feeds off the environment of surveillance in which we live.

THE ROLE OF TECHNOLOGY

Technology inevitably becomes the focus of most discussions about privacy because it is the means by which individuals and institutions find out what they want about us. We must keep in mind that technology is just that: a means, and not the basic impulse for the invasions on our privacy. Still, technological innovations have undeniably made privacy invasions possible in ways never before envisioned. The problem is particularly acute because we often embrace new technologies with naive optimism before they are really understood. Privacy is being eroded because of cheap information, ignorance about new technology, technological glitches, and more intrusive surveillance.

Cheap Information

Once businesses and governments had to keep all records on paper. But the bureaucratic days of filling out forms in triplicate and dusty rooms filled with filing cabinets are long over. Information is much less expensively and far more efficiently stored, and it is much more accessible. Not long ago, someone seeking information about an individual had to phone the proper institution and cajole or bribe an employee to dig up a physical record. Now databases can be accessed without any need to interact with other people, and duplicate information can be stored in a laptop computer. In addition, different pieces of data about a person can be merged together almost effortlessly to form a single, exhaustive profile.

Ignorance About New Technology

A widespread lack of understanding of new technology is another cause of the problem. The way we use e-mail is a good example of this. When you send mail through the post office, you put it in an opaque envelope and seal it shut. Why? Because you want the contents to remain private—you don't want someone other than the intended recipient reading your mail. But with e-mail, most people are doing exactly what they would never do with regular mail. Few realize how easily a third party can read their e-mail.

This widespread naiveté often prevents possible technological solutions to these problems from working effectively. Consider this statement from Kevin Railsback, the West Coast technical director of the InfoWorld Test Center:

> For some time now, I've been using [e-mail] security products such as PGP (Pretty Good Privacy) and its open-source version, GPGP (Gnome PGP). I have a public key, and I have the public keys of a few friends, but the technology isn't too useful for everyday use. The basic problem is that until a critical mass understands how public its information really is on the Internet and decides that privacy is important enough to protect, then the majority won't use the technology. Public key encryption, the building block that PGP and such products are built on, has been around for years. It works great, makes your e-mail virtually impossible to break in to, and isn't that tough to set up.[10]

Technological Glitches

With all of the technological advances in data storage and transmission, glitches can now mistakenly make public all sorts of personal data. On September 15, 2000, for example, First Virginia Bank's online service allowed customers to view other people's account information, including deposits, balances, and cleared checks.[11] In this case, the glitch did not affect actual balances or reveal personal identities. But earlier in the year NetBank had sent a slip to one customer containing another customer's personal information, including his Social Security number. And as CNET News.com reported, H&R Block "shut down its online tax filing service after the company accidentally exposed some customers' sensitive financial records to other customers."[12]

More Intrusive Surveillance

A New Zealand man confessed in court to nine counts of using his "shoe-cam" to take video footage up the skirts of thousands of unsuspecting women and girls at public events. The device was unnoticeable on his shoe, linked by a wire running up the leg of his pants. The man then loaded these images on his computer and posted them on the Internet.[13] This is but one example of the avalanche of new technologies: video cameras that fit on a shirt button; audio receivers that can be inserted seamlessly into a telephone, a fountain pen, or a potted plant; scanners that can pluck telephone conversations out of the air and effortlessly trace them to their source; and much more.

Not only can criminals use these technological innovations, but governments and businesses can use them as well.

THE REAL CULPRIT AND THE REAL COST

Just a month after Amy Boyer's death, *Forbes* magazine ran a cover story on the lack of privacy in our society. Although the story was unrelated to the Boyer case, it featured Docusearch.com—the company that enabled Liam Youens to track down his victim. *Forbes* writer Adam L. Penenberg dared Dan Cohn, the head of Docusearch.com, to dig up all the information the investigator could find about him, starting with nothing but his name. Two days later Cohn had discovered Penenberg's birth date, his mother's maiden name, his address, and his Social Security number. (Cohn said it took him only five minutes of actual investigation.) Penenberg was even more shocked at what Cohn was able to dig up in less than a week. He wrote: "In all of six days Dan Cohn and his Web detective agency, Docusearch.com, shattered every notion I had about privacy in this country (or whatever remains of it). Using only a keyboard and the phone, he was able to uncover the innermost details of my life—whom I call late at night; how much money I have in the bank; my salary and rent. He even got my unlisted phone numbers, both of them."[14]

People are justifiably outraged at Docusearch's role in Youens's murderous actions. But while Docusearch and other investigative services profit from the destruction of our privacy, they are not the ones primarily responsible for it. Indeed, it is all too easy simply to blame such companies—or government, or big business—for our present situation. But the fact is that we have enjoyed many of the benefits of the information revolution without really counting the cost. As cartoonist Walt Kelly wrote in *Pogo*, "We have met the enemy and he is us."[15]

Until we acknowledge that we are responsible for our present situation and have willingly exchanged our privacy for convenience or comfort, we will not take the steps necessary to regain control of our privacy—or our lives.

We have lost power over our lives because we want to enjoy the convenience offered us, because we try to exercise control over our lives. We are open to dealing with anyone who has a way of bringing us something quickly, conveniently, or cheaply—but in exchange for a little information.

Because of the convenience we gain, we tend to celebrate uncritically every technological innovation, be it e-mail, the Web, or whatever. As technology critic Neil Postman points out: "It is a mistake to suppose that any technological innovation has a one-sided effect. Every technology is both a burden and a blessing; not either-or, but both-and. Nothing could be more obvious, of course, especially to those who have given more than two minutes of thought to the matter. Nonetheless, we are currently surrounded by throngs of ... one-eyed prophets who see only what new technologies can do and are incapable of imagining what they will *undo*. They gaze on technology as a lover does on his beloved, seeing it as without blemish and entertaining no apprehension for the future."[16]

We are so content with the blessings we receive from the new technologies that we fail to realize just how much of our privacy we are giving away.

CONCLUSION

We are being tracked. Vast amounts of personal information are being collected and stored. The question is: Can we do anything about it?

We can—if we take the initiative. In fact, until more people are willing to show by their actions—by the way they live, communicate, and budget their money—that they value their privacy, no reforms in government, or in business, or in law enforcement, are likely to do much good. We can and must protect our privacy, and this book is written to show you how to do it.

But first we need to know what we're up against.

CHAPTER TWO

CORPORATE SPIES

The same computer technologies that slash costs from the retail distribution chain, and deliver individualized suggestions for books or music, can help create an invisible, indelible and seemingly inescapable trail of personal information.

—WALL STREET JOURNAL

The chairman of a major fund drive proudly reported that he and his people knew everything about their target donors "except which hand they brush their teeth with."[1] How do fund-raisers learn so much about those whom they approach for money? Do they hire private investigators? Do they spy?

Somehow they *do* gather a great deal of information about their potential benefactors. Indeed, according to Philip Herrera, the executive director of *Town & Country* magazine, those who rely on philanthropy take seriously the need to hunt for a philanthropist:

"Virtually all the best universities, hospitals, conservation groups and arts institutions have departments devoted to the cultivation of generous donors. And increasingly, those departments include one or more 'prospect researchers' who know how to prowl the Internet, collecting and collating existing data about you."[2]

The Web is crucial because records that formerly were only on paper and had to be gathered by phone calls are now accessible to anyone with a computer and a modem. Someone can assemble all sorts of information about your life in order to improve his chances of getting something from you. Herrera writes:

> Christopher Hughes, head of prospect research at the Metropolitan Museum of Art, explains that he initiates a search with Lexis-Nexis Universe, an expensive, on-line subscriber service Web site that has "tons of databases," including articles in dozens of newspapers and magazines. If the prospect is a businessman, Hughes will also search SEC filings (proxy statements, 10-K quarterly reports, etc.) for stock holdings and personal information. If the target is a lawyer, his law firm's Web site and its listing in the Martindale-Hubbell on-line directory will provide some biographical background. Magazine Web sites, like www.forbes.com and www.fortune.com, might contain articles mentioning the prospect's outside interests and hobbies. And if he is a generous donor to charity, the Foundation Center in New York City will yield yet more information (on CD-ROM).[3]

The search will then continue while all your past employments and groups have been tracked down so that the researcher has a profile on which to base decisions about how to approach you and how much you are likely to give.

According to Herrera, though such an investigation "may seem to border on invasion of privacy, it doesn't." Why not? *Because all the information is in the public domain.* He also assures us that such researchers for charities abide by an ethic of extreme confidentiality.

Well. The fact remains that the way "prospect researchers" are able to operate demonstrates that privacy is quickly coming to an end. Even if these practices are not technically a violation of confidential information, people need to be aware of how easy it now is for strangers to control them.

KNOWLEDGE AND CONTROL

Have you ever had a friend who could get you to do things that he wanted you to do? Because he knows all about you, he is able to talk you into things you hadn't thought of doing. No big deal, right? After all, he is your friend, and you trust him.

But it is a big deal now that someone working for a political campaign or a college or a charity can basically do the same thing. Fund-raisers, marketers, and the like learn the intimate details of our lives because they believe by doing so they can get us to serve their needs.

Recall how quickly and easily Docusearch.com investigator Dan Cohn tracked down deeply personal information about Adam Penenberg of *Forbes*—Social Security number, address, birth date, utility bills, unlisted phone numbers, bank account balances, direct deposits, ATM usage, check numbers with dates and amounts, the name of his broker. Cohn did all this completely legally, even though it involved misrepresenting himself on the phone (private detectives call this a "pretext").[4]

Some make the case that we are all better off with less privacy in the business world. For instance, David Boaz, the vice president of the libertarian Cato Institute, has commented, "There's a positive value to being offered things that will interest you, and it's hardly something to be feared."5 Still, so-called consumer preferences are being collected at an alarming rate, crossing the line into manipulation and control. And many people simply are not aware of how often their information is shared, intentionally or unintentionally. Companies can violate or suddenly change their own privacy policies. They can accidentally send out your personal information. They can neglect security so that your information is readily accessible. Sometimes they use or share their information about you to defraud you. And sometimes, as we saw in the last chapter, someone may use this information to steal your identity or stalk you.

Addressing the issue of the end of privacy, Adam Penenberg asks the right question: "You may well ask: What's the big deal? We consumers are as much to blame as marketers for all these loose data. At every turn we have willingly given up a layer of privacy in exchange for convenience; it is why we use a credit card to shop, enduring a barrage of junk mail. Why should we care if our personal information isn't so personal anymore? Well, take this test: Next time you are at a party, tell a stranger your salary, checking account balance, mortgage payment and Social Security number. If this makes you uneasy, you have your answer."6

Breaking Promises

Even if we don't need new laws regulating privacy, it would be nice to see prosecutors holding businesses accountable when they violate their agreements with customers by revealing information they had promised to keep confidential. The fact that this happens so often indicates that businesses can get away with ignoring promises in which customers put their trust.

The Disney-backed online company Toysmart.com made a pledge of privacy to its customers, promising not to share its database with other companies. The pledge read in part: "Our promise: At Toysmart.com, we take great pride in our relationships with our customers and pledge to maintain your privacy while visiting our site. Personal information voluntarily submitted by visitors to our site, such as name, address, billing information, and shopping preferences, is never shared with a third-party...."[7] Then the company went bankrupt and, as *Wired News* reported, "promptly put its customer database, one of its most valuable and liquid assets, up for sale."[8]

Toysmart.com is not unique. According to TRUSTe, a non-profit privacy watchdog, other dot-coms are doing this all the time, promising privacy and then selling their customer databases when they go bankrupt. For example, Boo.com and Epidemic.com also sold information they had promised to keep private.[9]

Perhaps the controversy over Toysmart.com prompted Amazon.com to state its intentions openly so that no one could accuse it of breaking promises. In September 2000 the online retailer announced that it was changing its policy: Amazon now explicitly states that information about customers is an asset that can be sold if the company goes out of business. The new policy also states that this might also happen during the course of regular business: "As we continue to develop our business, we might sell or buy stores or assets. In such transactions, customer information generally is one of the transferred business assets."[10] No longer can customers opt out of having their information shared with marketing companies or partner retailers. As a result, two major privacy groups have broken their association with Amazon.[11]

Ambiguous Promises

Most people want a promise of privacy from companies they associate with. But even when such promises are in place, it is sometimes difficult to know what exactly they mean and how much they protect the consumer. As I write this, online retailer More.com is defending itself in court because a third party received customer information that the company had promised to keep private. An investigator in the Missouri attorney general's office tried unsuccessfully to order contact lenses from More.com under an assumed name; shortly thereafter he received a solicitation for the assumed name from Lens Express, Inc.—even though he'd given that name only to More.com. It turns out that the online retailer used Lens Express to fulfill its orders, and apparently Lens Express used the information for its own purposes. In this case, More.com's policy does state that it uses third parties as fulfillment partners to provide health products, and the company probably met its promise to its customers.[12]

Nevertheless, the More.com case shows how ambiguous privacy promises can be, and ultimately the incident reveals how difficult it is to keep your personal information from spreading. Compounding the problem is the fact that at present there is no legal definition of privacy. No one in government or business can seem to agree on what privacy really means.[13]

Until there is widespread agreement about what information can and should be protected, and how that should be protected, we cannot rely on others to ensure our privacy. Information will be available to anyone unless and until individuals take the initiative to reclaim their privacy.

Lacking Concern

While many businesses wish to profit from the information they've gathered from you, it seems some businesses simply aren't motivated to keep your personal data confidential. A man in Ohio criticized his company superiors under a pseudonym in a Yahoo!

PRACTICAL PRIVACY TIP #1:
Protect Your Privacy on the Information Superhighway

Jayne Hitchcock, an advocate for victims of cyberstalking,[14] offers some tips to avoiding the kind of harassment she and many others have suffered:

1. Use an e-mail name that is gender neutral, doesn't draw too much curiosity, and doesn't give away information that could identify you.

2. Use a free e-mail account like those found at Hotbot.com or Lycos.com. Use it for all posting on bulletin boards, Web purchasing, and other such activities. Give anyone you don't know only this e-mail address, if any.

3. Before getting involved in chat rooms or newsgroups, observe for a while in order to get a feel for who is participating.

4. In public forums enter only those messages that you would say to someone's face.

5. Every once in a while, put your own name into search engines and see if anything comes up. Find out if you're being talked about.[15]

chat room. The company produced a civil subpoena, and Yahoo! revealed his identity without ever notifying him that his identity was being sought. The man lost his job because he had assumed his privacy would be protected. In this case, Yahoo! learned something—it now states that it will inform a person if another party is seeking his identity in a civil action and will give him fifteen days to take legal steps if he wishes. Yahoo!'s newer policy reflects common sense: you should have some appeal to the law before your personal information is given to a third party intending to take action against you.[16] Unfortunately, such sense is not common enough among businesses, and our privacy is threatened as a result.

Worse still, a survey of e-businesses revealed that customer privacy was at the *bottom* of their priorities; their own security came at the top. A consultant with the company that sponsored the survey commented, "From that, it's pretty obvious that businesses are concerned about being hacked or being exposed to the public, but aren't so sensitive about protecting customer data."[17]

In the case of employees, companies can be worse than apathetic about privacy; they sometimes act as if workers don't have any.[18] More and more we are seeing employers actually spying on their workers, to the point that many invasive tactics are now considered de rigueur. In my day job I am an executive with a large, publicly held publishing company. Recently our Information Technology department announced that it would be providing managers with detailed monthly reports of their employees' Internet usage: what sites they had visited, how often, and for how long. As far as I know, I was the only manager to raise an objection. Everyone else accepted this provision as a welcome management tool.

Accidents Happen—and Happen and Happen

We can also see how low a priority customer privacy is to businesses when we consider how often they accidentally disseminate our information. On September 9, 2000, About.com mistakenly revealed the e-mail addresses of more than twelve hundred of its customers to all of its Sprinks.com clients. The company immediately acknowledged its mistake and asked everyone on the e-mail list not to use the other addresses. But one customer responded: "When a company does something like this it really makes you question the competence of the people they are hiring and the training (or lack of training they give them). You trust these people

PRACTICAL PRIVACY TIP #2:
Understand How Your Boss Can Snoop on You

More and more employers are monitoring their workers on the job. In fact, according to the American Management Association, nearly three-quarters of U.S. companies now electronically monitor employees in one way or another.[19] Much of this surveillance is legal, so in order to protect your privacy in the workplace, you need to know what your boss is looking at. Some companies are now using hidden video cameras and other sophisticated surveillance gadgets, but here I will cover only what employers most commonly monitor: e-mail, Internet, and telephone usage.[20]

E-mail

Any time you use e-mail you should be careful about what you send, but you should be particularly cautious when you are e-mailing at work. In general, employers are within their rights to monitor what is sent and received on their own e-mail systems. In some cases employees have been fired for e-mails they sent—for making offensive comments (e.g., racist remarks, sexual harassment), disparaging supervisors, revealing company secrets, and more. Of course, e-mail and the Internet are still relatively new, so many of the legal questions about employees' right to privacy with these technologies are unresolved. For now, it's best to assume that your boss can monitor (and is monitoring) your e-mails and to exercise caution accordingly. Don't send any message that you wouldn't want your boss or a coworker to see.

One caveat: never assume that an e-mail is gone once you delete it. Not only does the recipient/sender probably still have a copy, but also many companies have automatic backup systems that copy all messages as they are sent or received.

Internet

For the most part, your employer can monitor your Internet usage: what sites you visit, how often, and for how long. As with e-mail, most employers stipulate that their Internet connection is not for employees' personal use. There have been famous cases in which employees were dismissed for downloading pornographic material on company computers. Again, your best bet is to assume that your employer can and will monitor you at work. Be careful about how you use the Internet.

Telephone

If you're on the phone at work, your boss can listen in. Your voice mail is similarly subject to monitoring. Employers own the phone system, so they can generally monitor it as they see fit. Your boss can keep a record of the numbers you dial and how long you talk, and can listen to your voice-mail messages. (As with e-mail, never assume that a voice-mail message is gone just because you've erased it; your company could have the message saved in its system.) Technically, the Electronic Communications Privacy Act prevents companies from listening to employees' personal calls, but if you want to have a truly private conversation, you should probably conduct it outside of the workplace.

with private information and the next thing you know it's all over the Internet."[21]

E-mail addresses aren't the worst information to be sent out accidentally, but such mishaps should make people realize how easy it would be for much more damaging personal information to be disseminated to others.

Dan Huddle, the chief technology officer for Xanga.com, reported that when he attempted to order a catalog online from IKEA, he received an error message with a file name in it.

Entering the file name into the Web address, he found himself looking at a database of information about customers who had ordered from the IKEA catalog—their names, addresses, phone numbers, and e-mail addresses. According to Chris Christiansen, an analyst and security expert at International Data Corporation, this was not a unique occurrence. He said he had seen this sort of mistake happen at other Web sites that didn't make security of customer data a priority.[22]

While one might think IKEA made the mistake because it was new to the Internet, one can't say the same for Amazon.com, which was reported at the same time to have exposed users' e-mail addresses to members of its Associates program. According to *ComputerWorld* magazine: "Associates customer Dave English said that when he logged into Amazon.com's Associates' page ... he discovered that Amazon accidentally exposed other users' e-mail addresses to him. 'If you go to the Amazon Associates program log-in page and choose to have it e-mail you your password, it complains that the e-mail address you entered is invalid [even if it is fine]. Then if you hit the refresh button, you can end up seeing other e-mail addresses of other folks trying to retrieve their password as well.' "[23] Though the company said it was fixing the problem, days later English found he could still view the e-mail addresses. He pointed out that it would have been easy for a customer to write a program that kept refreshing the screen and storing the e-mails.

Commenting on the situation to *ComputerWorld*, Andrew Shen of the Electronic Privacy Information Center (EPIC) in Washington stated the obvious: "When [customers] provide personal information to a company's Web site, they expect that information to be protected. There's no such thing as perfect security, but you have to respond quickly rather than later.

Amazon has a responsibility to fix the problem as soon as possible and tell customers what happened."[24] Shen also noted that companies have little incentive to make privacy a priority. There are no legal penalties for failing to respond in a timely way to a privacy breach.

Eve.com is another company that accidentally exposed customer information. On September 13, 2000, simply by entering a number in the URL someone could learn a customer's name, address, what he had ordered and when, the type of credit card used, and the last five digits of the card number. To its credit the company shut down its Web site as soon as it learned of the problem, but before it did, Eve.com's entire customer history was publicly available.[25]

Virtually the same problem occurred at Netmarket.com about a year and a half earlier. The site exposed customer orders to anyone who entered random numbers, providing names and addresses along with the customers' purchase histories. Just a month previously, CNET News.com had reported that at least a hundred small sites, as well as big ones such as Yahoo!, Excite, and AT&T, had exposed private information. After the Netmarket.com glitch, Ken Allard, a site operations manager at Jupiter Communications, told CNET that Web users should expect more of these sorts of problems in the near future—a prediction borne out by the subsequent glitches at Amazon.com, Eve.com, and IKEA.[26]

To be sure, this problem is not unique to American companies. Clicksure, a company that certifies Web sites, conducted a survey of major European health-care companies that used the Internet. It found that

- 70 percent of them stored the personal data of customers in a potentially unsafe environment that could be hacked;

- 67 percent did not give their customers the right to with-hold private information;
- 44 percent made it impossible for customers to complete a transaction without disclosing unnecessary details;
- 31 percent did not tell customers if their personal information would be passed on to another company;
- 28 percent did not have any policy regarding privacy.[27]

Plainly, too much of our information is being collected in unsecured locations. But even secured locations can make mistakes. Western Union once had to go offline because someone had hacked into its computer and stolen the credit or debit card information of 15,700 customers. Apparently programmers, during the course of routine maintenance on the site, accidentally left the data unprotected.[28]

PREDATORS

Of course, as soon as Western Union learned of the problem, it shut down its Internet site and informed those whose data had been stolen. But other corporations are not so ethical. In September 2000 the Federal Trade Commission won a $37.5 million verdict against an X-rated Web site because the site had acquired the credit card information of three million people and billed them for services never rendered. These people had never visited the Web site; thousands of them didn't even own a computer. The company managed to operate several fake businesses, so as soon as customer complaints roused the suspicions of the credit card company, a different business would do the billing. Customers saw a different company billing them every month—names they had never seen before.[29]

Though it is perhaps not shocking that a porn company would try to rip people off, it is important to realize where the company got the credit card numbers: from a bank.[30] In fact, it is quite common for a bank to sell customers' personal financial information to another company. Usually this doesn't result in outright credit card fraud, but it does mean that the telemarketer calling you has more information at his disposal than you probably realize. The story of U.S. Bancorp in the last chapter is not atypical. In fact, MemberWorks, the telemarketing company that paid U.S. Bancorp for the data, has worked with seventeen of the twenty-five largest banks.[31]

Indeed, there is virtually no enforceable privacy for bank customers. Syndicated columnist Jane Bryant Quinn reported:

> Theoretically, the Fair Credit Reporting Act (FCRA) limits the way some of your financial records can be used. FCRA covers credit information—for example, your income, assets and employment history. Under the law, banks have to tell you that they might disclose this information, and give you a chance to take your name off the telemarketing lists. This is called "opting out." Unfortunately, there's no effective way of enforcing FCRA, says [Comptroller of the Currency John D.] Hawke, whose office regulates 2,400 national banks. The regulators don't know what the banks are doing, and few customers know they can opt out. What's more, no federal law protects what's called "transaction and experience" information—namely, the details of your bank and credit card accounts. They can be disclosed to telemarketers at will, says Amy Friend, assistant chief counsel at the Office of the Comptroller of the Currency. So can your Social Security number.[32]

U.S. Bancorp, once it was caught, agreed not to work with *nonfinancial* telemarketers. But it is still free to share your information with a company wanting to sell financial products.[33]

ALL EYES ON US

If you go to the Web site ClaritasExpress.com, you can enter a zip code and receive profiles of the kinds of people that live in your area. The site advertises that you can find out about the "lifestyle of the people who live in your neighborhood," the "propensity of your customers to purchase specific goods and services," and the "demographics of your market area."[34] Many of the services are free. For example, you can find out, based on 1990 census data, that people who live within the 14744 zip code, in western New York's Allegheny County, are mostly "Gray Power" (likely to belong to a country club or watch the Travel Channel), "New Eco-topia" (forty-five-year-olds and older who are likely to go skiing), "Grain Belt" (likely to own a cat and go hunting), "Blue Highways" (likely to watch Court TV and do furniture refinishing), and "Hard Scrabble" (likely to use coupons for tobacco and watch auto racing on TV).

And this information is just a free sample. A business could purchase full services to obtain much more detailed information broken up according to nine-digit area codes.

Obviously, if you could simply protect your phone and mailbox from marketers—which I will show you how to do—you would be immune to most of this. But a site like ClaritasExpress demonstrates the powerful desire of corporations to collect information on you—information that can then be abused either by the business or by someone else who gets access to it.

You need to take steps to reduce that risk.

CHAPTER THREE

ROGUE PREDATORS

It's actually obscene what you can find out about a person.

—Liam Youens

When Michelle returned home from a Mexican vacation, she was stopped by U.S. Customs officials who accused her of crimes she had not committed. The DEA had put out notice that it was looking for her on drug-related charges. As far as the agents were concerned, she was a fugitive.

Michelle was not caught entirely by surprise. She had known for some time that she was the victim of identity theft. A woman had stolen her personal information and assumed her identity, impersonating her even though the two looked nothing alike. As a preventative measure Michelle had brought with her to Mexico documents proving that her identity had been stolen, including

court filings and police records. She wanted to be sure she was prepared in case a Customs computer flagged her as a criminal.

It made almost no difference. She testified to the Senate:

> I was held … for an hour while I explained the circumstances
> of my erroneous link with [the thief's] criminal record…. As I pre-
> sented endless documentation of court records, police filings, etc.,
> and explained my situation in a stream of tears, I knew then that
> I had become erroneously linked with [the thief's] criminal
> record. The agents questioned my story and documentation, and
> treated me very suspiciously—like I was the criminal. After the
> police detective was called and vouched for me, I was allowed to
> leave. I feared being arrested or being taken into custody. I found
> out later that … the DEA posted a lookout for "me" in the system.
> They neglected to let me know that I might want to be prepared
> for this type of confusion at any time.[1]

Ironically, the identity thief had already been incarcerated for
the charges leveled against Michelle.

EVIL TWIN

For Michelle this had been an ongoing nightmare. More than
a year earlier her identity had been stolen, and it would be many
more months before she would be able to clear her name. She presented the Senate Subcommittee on Technology, Terrorism, and
Government Information with a synopsis of what she had endured:

- January 1998—The identity thief steals Michelle's rental
  application from a property management office.
- February 1998—The thief sets up a wireless phone account
  and has it billed to a new address.

- March 1998—The thief sets up a landline phone at a new residence. This lasts four months, and she fails to pay almost $1,500 in bills.

- October 1998—The thief acquires a duplicate driver's license with her own picture and a different residence.

- December 1998—The thief acquires a zero-down lease under Michelle's name for a $32,000 Dodge Ram pickup and, using Michelle's identity, goes $3,400 in debt for liposuction.

- January 1999—When a bank calls about the truck, Michelle finally discovers that her Social Security number has been used to steal her identity. She puts fraud alerts out to all credit reporting agencies and on her driver's license number, cancels her credit cards, and puts heightened security on her bank accounts. A police detective finds out the thief's pager number and, after she responds to a page, tells her to turn herself in. Instead, she flees.

- May 1999—The thief identifies herself as Michelle when arrested and charged with trafficking three thousand pounds of marijuana. Authorities never notice the flag on the license number, and the thief is set free. Michelle now has a criminal record.

- July 1999—The police catch the thief and book her on drug charges, among other things. She identifies herself to the police as "Michelle Brown," and she is incarcerated under that name.

- September 1999—The thief is sentenced at the state level to three concurrent two-year terms for perjury, grand theft, and possession of stolen property. Meanwhile, when Michelle returns from Mexico, law enforcement officials accost her at Los Angeles International Airport.

- October/November 1999—The thief is transferred to Chicago Federal Prison as "Michelle Brown" and uses Michelle's name in her return address in prison. The district attorney promises to correct the matter.
- June 2000—The thief is sentenced to seventy-three months for the three thousand pounds of marijuana and for lying to a federal judge.[2]

Still, Michelle had no real assurance that her name and reputation were truly restored. She described to the Senate the harrowing experience of identity theft:

> Through the course of uncovering [the thief's] trail and waiting for her to be caught, I honestly believed that the victimization would never end, that I would never become whole again as the true "Michelle Brown." My world had become a living nightmare. I personally was affected extremely: I was significantly distracted at a job that I had just started three weeks prior to the day of discovery. I suffered from a nearly nonexistent appetite, very little sleep, and was consumed with the ferocious chore of restoring my name and attempting to quell any future abuse.... No words will ever be strong enough to completely convince others what this period was like, filled with terror, aggravation, unceasing anger, and frustration.... I still fear what might happen as I cross the U.S. border, and I cannot get assurance from any governmental agency that this situation will never happen again.[3]

YOUR VULNERABLE GOOD NAME

Michelle is not alone. In order to have access to our information, a network of government agencies and corporations has produced an environment in which you and I are vulnerable to anyone who wishes to victimize us. According to *USA Today* financial columnist Sandra Block, complaints to the Federal Trade Commission through its Identity Theft hotline *tripled* in the six months from March to September 1999.[4] The government estimates that a half-million people are victims of identity theft each year.[5]

Easy Info

"This is the information age, and information is power! Discover the secrets of the people with whom you associate. Enter, because what you don't know, can hurt you." So reads the copy on the Web page of Docusearch.com. On the site you can choose between various search categories: Locate, Driver and Vehicle, Telephone, Financial, Criminal, Property, and Civil. Here are some things you can click and buy—just like shopping on Amazon.com:

- Locate by name: $39
- Current address from phone number: $49[6]
- Statewide driver history by name and license: $39
- Bank account search and bank account balance search: $49 and $249, respectively
- Bank account activity detail: $99
- Property records by name and by address: $39 and $33, respectively

In the aftermath of the Ann Boyer stalking case, Docusearch.com says it will no longer reveal Social Security numbers, and for some searches the client must provide an explanation for why he wants certain information. But, despite Docusearch's new policy, as long as Social Security numbers show up on public documents they are still fair game. Thus at Digdirt.com, a marriage record search (available in five states) or a divorce search (available in six) may provide a Social Security number.[7] And other companies still offer to give you someone's Social Security number for a fee. I did a Yahoo! search and found I could get a Social Security number simply by punching in the name and last known address and paying $47.70 to Nationwide-Detective.com.[8] Likewise, SSNTrace-search.com offers three types of background searches, saying: "These three searches are great to run if you want to find out about a person's background. There are three types, and each type returns different amounts of information. These are excellent as pre-employment checks or to just 'find out some info' on someone."[9] Two of these three searches include a person's Social Security number. If you simply want to "find out some info" on someone, there it is for the taking.

Can something be done about this? In 1999 Congress passed the Gramm-Leach-Bliley Act, which supposedly made the theft of financial information illegal and punishable. Writing in *Newsbytes*, Brian Krebbs reported the result of the legislation:

> A survey conducted over the summer recess by the House Banking Committee found that, despite privacy protections passed in last year's financial services modernization bill, a slew of companies advertising on the Internet and in the backs of newspapers and legal publications continue to offer financial information about virtually anyone for a marginal fee. At a hearing on identity theft and other financial privacy issues today, House Banking Committee Chairman James A. Leach, R-Iowa, said committee staff contacted businesses found on the Internet and in legal trade journals advertising the ability to locate bank accounts, account balances, and other financial information most consumers would consider confidential. All eleven of the companies randomly contacted confirmed their ability and willingness

---

PRACTICAL PRIVACY TIP #3:
Protect Yourself Against Identity Theft

USA Today financial columnist Sandra Block gave her readers some helpful tips to protect themselves against identity theft. To summarize:

1. Talk to your employer about how your personal information is being protected. Workplaces are very profitable places for identity thieves.

2. Refrain from giving personal financial information over a cordless phone or a cellular. The older the model the more the risk that criminals might be able to listen in on your message with a scanner.

3. Get government checks—whether Social Security, IRS refunds, or anything else—deposited electronically.

4. Get a credit report from one of the three credit reporting agencies once a year.

5. Destroy all preapproved offers from credit card companies.

6. When selecting a password for extra security on your credit accounts, choose something other than your mother's maiden name.[10]

---

to collect a broad range of financial information on a particular individual for a fee. Leach said the brief, three-hour survey demonstrated that consumer protections included in the passage of last year's Gramm-Leach-Bliley Act have done little to discourage would-be information brokers. One amendment included in the bill makes it a federal crime to obtain customer information from a financial institution under false pretenses, such as misrepresenting one's identity.[11]

Plainly, people who want to use your identity, your money, or your reputation—as it is reflected in your credit—can rather easily gather sensitive personal and financial information about you. If you are a victim, your good name will be smeared, as credit agencies and other institutions—perhaps even law enforcement agencies—bear down on *you*, thinking you are the perpetrator.

In many cases, law enforcement agencies think they are looking for different people who have committed different crimes, only to realize later that they are looking for one person who assumed several identities. In the case of one identity thief, Jamie Paul Pittman, the *Oregonian* reported:

> Pittman was opening bank accounts under several identities—usually with stolen driver's licenses and Social Security numbers. With those, he was able to deposit stolen or forged high-dollar checks, withdrawing some or all of the money before the check cleared.
>
> Every month or so, he'd move onto a new alias and a new checking account. According to court papers, he spent lots of the money living the high life.
>
> The cops were onto him. Sort of.
>
> "The FBI was investigating one alias, and the Secret Service was investigating another," said Charles Gorder, an assistant U.S. attorney in Portland. "They didn't know it was the same guy."[12]

Credit agencies and financial institutions can seemingly do little to stop this crime from happening over and over again. Shon Bouldon of Hillsboro, Oregon, had his Social Security number shared among twelve identity thieves, who used his name and credit history to open bank accounts, secure car loans, and open retail accounts. He did what he was supposed to do: he alerted the

PRACTICAL PRIVACY TIP #4:
Ten Ways to Avoid Becoming the Victim of Credit Card Fraud

According to the Federal Trade Commission, your liability for unauthorized charges to your credit card is only $50.[15] But there are other costs involved, most notably your time—it can take weeks, months, or even years to get the whole mess straightened out. You can greatly reduce your chances of becoming a victim by observing these rules:

1. Never sign the back of your credit cards. Instead, write "Ask for photo ID." Do this immediately upon receiving the card.

2. Retain your copy of the receipt. Compare it to your statement and then shred it.

3. Open your credit card statements promptly and reconcile them, just as you would your checking account.

4. Immediately dispute in writing any questionable charges. If you suspect fraud, notify the "big three" credit bureaus—Equifax, Experian (formerly TRW), and Trans Union—and have them flag your account with a "fraud alert."

5. Request copies of your credit report from each of the three credit bureaus. Look for suspicious entries.

6. Do not lend your credit cards to anyone. Also, do not leave your credit cards lying around.

7. Do not leave your credit card statements or payments in an unlocked mailbox. They can easily be stolen.

8. Never give out your credit card number over the phone or in an e-mail message.

9. Record your credit card numbers, passwords or PINs, and toll-free numbers and store the information in a secure environment.

10. If you lose your credit cards or suspect that they've been stolen, immediately report the loss to each company.

credit reporting agencies and had them put fraud alerts on his accounts. It didn't do much good. People have continued opening accounts under his name. "I fear every day that I won't be able to get this fixed and that I'll have bad credit for my whole life," he said.[13]

Of course, amid all the concern about identity theft, we need to remember there is also run-of-the-mill credit card fraud. Especially over the Internet, where purchasing is expected to be so impersonal, it is easy to order something with a stolen credit card. Complicating this issue is the growing phenomenon of consumers' purchasing with their own credit cards and then claiming they never ordered (or, alternately, never received) the merchandise.[14]

Stalking and Cyberstalking

Amy Boyer's murder is a stark reminder that identity theft, troublesome as it is, is not the only risk. Other, perhaps more violent kinds of criminals can find out virtually anything they want about you and use it against you. Stalking, for one, is indeed a real problem.

With the Internet, however, we now have a new concern: cyberstalking. In this case all the perpetrator needs is your primary e-mail address, and you will find your heart beating with fear every time you hear your computer say, "You've got mail." An estimated thirty thousand cases of cyberstalking are reported each year.[16]

In Los Angeles, a man assumed the online identity of a woman who had scorned his romantic advances. Using her e-mail address, he went to Web sites and posted messages confessing rape fantasies. He also gave out her address and other identifiers in online private forums. The victim claimed she was visited and harassed by six men at various times.[17]

Another victim, Jayne Hitchcock, made the mistake of revealing in an online discussion group that a couple running a literary agency had tried to overcharge her. She was telling the truth; federal postal inspectors later charged the couple with mail fraud for running a scam, and the pair pleaded guilty. But that paled next to what Hitchcock has claimed they did to her. As Hitchcock reported in a civil suit against the couple, she first received hundreds of identical e-mails intended to jam her Internet connection. Next, an insulting message that Hitchcock had seemingly posted to an online discussion group provoked an explosion of angry e-mails. Then posts in her name began showing up on porn sites, soliciting sadomasochistic sex and giving out her address and phone number. According to Hitchcock, the couple also called her neighbors to get her new phone number when she had it changed.[18]

In another case, a cyberstalker doctored a picture of his victim to make a series of pornographic photos, which he then posted on a Web site with her name attached.[19]

Hacking Away at Your Privacy

Problems such as identity theft and stalking are compounded by the presence of computer hackers. As wonderful as computers are for data storage, many people find ways to break into them, whether for fun or for profit—or for both. In the fall of 2000, Radio Shack began distributing a product called CueCat, which scans information on magazines and newspapers in order to bring up corresponding Web sites. For the product to function, consumers had to register with DigitalConvergence, the company that made CueCat. The 140,000 people who did so through the company's Web site had their personal information hacked. CNET News.com quoted DigitalConvergence's vice president of new product development as saying, "For the people that registered via our Web site ... a hacker exploited a known error in the data script and was able to look into the data file. From there, they could extrapolate the name, e-mail address, age range, gender and Zip code of new members."[20]

In this case, hopefully the biggest risk was spam (unsolicited e-mail). But one can never be sure. Other hacking is much more dangerous and has become a real threat. For instance, computers have given a new face to corporate espionage. In fact, half of the six hundred companies surveyed by the Computer Security Institute said their competitors were probably responsible for cybercrime against them—claiming as a group to have lost some $60 million to computer espionage. In one case a man hacked into a competitor's file and then presented the work as his own. His superiors knew he wasn't capable of that sort of work, but they manufactured the product anyway.[21]

Hacking can also be an instrument of personal cyberstalking. According to *Time Digital*, a woman named Roxanne was settling down to chat online one afternoon when she noticed something was wrong. Other names showed up in her private chat room with her friend. Just as she was about to notify AOL, her computer screen spelled out, "Say goodbye, Roxanne," and then her computer shut down. No matter how many times Roxanne changed her password or blocked certain users, she kept encountering someone online who could take control of her computer and access her personal data.

It turned out that she had inadvertently downloaded a program called BackOrifice, which allowed the hacker to have remote control of her computer. She got rid of the program and is no longer harassed online, but she has never learned the identity of her cyberstalker.[22]

PRACTICAL PRIVACY TIP #5:
Six Things to Do If You Are Cyberstalked

Jayne Hitchcock also has advice for anyone who is being stalked online:

1. Keep records. The moment you realize what is going on, save everything on your computer in a special folder and print out a hard copy.
2. Ignore him. Do not respond to the cyberstalker.
3. Contact the harasser's Internet service provider (ISP).
4. Call your local police department.
5. Contact the State Police Computer Crimes Unit.
6. For support and help, contact the group Working to Halt Online Abuse (WHOA), of which Jayne Hitchcock is president, at www.haltabuse.org.[23]

CONCLUSION

Even if we could always trust the intentions of our government and of businesses with their use of our personal information, the fact remains that the ease with which we allow such information to be disseminated puts us at risk to other people—to stalkers and thieves, to hackers and anonymous investigators. We need to find a way to take back control of our lives.

CHAPTER FOUR
GOVERNMENT SURVEILLANCE

The American people must be willing to give up a degree of personal privacy in exchange for safety and security.
                              —FBI Director Louis Freeh

I n September 2000 a Global Privacy Summit was held in Washington, D.C. Participants included industry leaders from around the world, credit agency representatives, privacy advocates, and government spokesmen. Paul Thibodeau of *ComputerWorld* reported the consensus: "The most telling moment of this week's Global Privacy Summit here came in the final hour of the conference today when one of the participants, U.S. Federal Trade Commission (FTC) member Mozelle W. Thompson, asked the large audience of [business] representatives and privacy advocates a simple question: How many believe online privacy legislation is inevitable? A sea of hands were [*sic*] raised."[1]

When people understand what is happening to their privacy, they often clamor for the government to do something about it. But government is not the solution. In fact, it's a big part of the problem. No organization is more committed to the concept of total surveillance than the U.S. government.

A GROWING THREAT

Undoubtedly we would all be safer if we were each kept under constant surveillance. Criminals would be caught more readily, and many would think twice about committing crimes at all. If we all had to allow policemen in our homes regularly, illegal activity would be reduced dramatically.

But we don't live that way in America. We don't allow policemen to show up randomly at someone's home and burst in to ensure that the homeowner is not breaking the law. A police officer is first supposed to convince a judge to issue a search warrant on the grounds that the officer has "probable cause" to investigate. The Fourth Amendment to the Constitution, part of the Bill of Rights, guarantees this: "The right of the people to be secure in their persons, houses, papers, and effects, against unreasonable searches and seizures, shall not be violated, and no Warrants shall issue, but upon probable cause, supported by Oath or affirmation, and particularly describing the place to be searched, and the persons or things to be seized." Our founders paid dearly for the right to be free and secure from government intrusion. They intended to give us a government that respects privacy, but more and more it seems that privacy is slipping away.

Many claim that in order to have security we must give up at least some of our privacy. The fact is, however, that we need privacy in order to give us security. Without privacy no one will ever be safe.

To ask people to choose between privacy and security presupposes that those who have access to our data can always—or at least mostly—be trusted to keep us secure. But just as employers have used employees' personal data to exploit workers, so have government agents used their power to monitor people.

The government has long monitored its citizens through such low-tech devices as tax returns, driver's license data, and census polls. But increasingly it is deploying high-tech surveillance systems such as FinCEN, Echelon, and Carnivore to watch and eavesdrop in ways that are difficult to detect.

FinCEN

The front page of FinCEN's Web site reads: "The mission of the Financial Crimes Enforcement Network [FinCEN] is to support law enforcement investigative efforts and foster interagency and global cooperation against domestic and international financial crimes; and to provide U.S. policy makers with strategic analyses of domestic and worldwide money-laundering developments, trends and patterns. FinCEN works towards those ends through information collection, analysis, and sharing, technological assistance, and innovative and cost-effective implementation of Treasury authorities."

Translation: The government uses FinCEN to spy on us, to know everything about how we spend our money.

Actually, this isn't quite true. Really, our banks do the spying. The government requires it. Any transaction over $5,000, even "in aggregate," means that the bank must fill out an SAR (Suspicious Activities Report) if, as the law states, "the transaction has no business or apparent lawful purpose or is not the sort in which the particular customer would normally be expected to engage, and the bank knows of no reasonable explanation for the transaction after examining the available facts, including the background and possible purpose of the transaction."[2]

In other words, the government is requiring that banks be detectives. And the threshold for suspicion is awfully low. If you sell a used car or receive a gift from your parents, you might find yourself being investigated as a possible money launderer.

Even a publication that the law enforcement community relies on readily admits the radical nature of the above law. According to the *Money Laundering Alert*'s Web site,

> Under U.S. Bank Secrecy Act regulations that took effect on April 1, 1996, U.S. banks and other "depository institutions" are required to report "suspicious activity" to the U.S. government. The U.S. suspicious activity reporting system goes far beyond a mere new government form and transactions that involve only currency. For the first time, it requires those financial institutions to report more than just suspected money laundering activity or Bank Secrecy Act violations.
>
> A revolutionary aspect of the SAR rules is that they impose a duty on financial institutions to report ... suspicious activity, [which] covers all transactions that are conducted or attempted "by, at, or through" the reporting institution.[3]

FinCEN is well connected to covert agencies, including the Central Intelligence Agency (CIA).[4] Indeed, the current director of FinCEN, James Sloan, previously served in the Secret Service and on the National Security Council's Counter-Terrorism Security Group. With these connections FinCEN can retrieve financial information from various databases to find money launderers—or those who engage in any behavior the government regards as suspicious.

Writing in *Wired* magazine, journalist Anthony Kimery acknowledged the serious threat this poses to our privacy:

> "There are legitimate concerns" regarding privacy, a ranking House banking committee staffer conceded in an interview with *Wired*. "Quite frankly, there hasn't been much congressional oversight with respect to the intelligence community's involvement with FinCEN. When you start trying to look into this, you start running up against all kinds of roadblocks." The GAO official involved in auditing FinCEN agreed that questions regarding the intelligence community's involvement and attendant privacy concerns haven't been addressed. If such issues have been the subject of discussion behind the closed doors of the House and Senate intelligence committees, no one is talking openly about it. Meanwhile, the potential for abusive intrusion by government into the financial affairs of private citizens and businesses is growing almost unnoticed and unchecked.[5]

Kimery was writing in 1993, but the threat is just as potent today. In his article Kimery mentioned the possibility of a Deposit Tracking System—quite simply a way to track every bank deposit in the country; not surprisingly, several intelligence agencies were in favor of it. While this wildly intrusive measure still has not been implemented, legislators are making similar proposals all the time. For example, in 1999 a Federal Reserve official proposed a new technology whereby currency would register itself every time it was deposited and would track how long it had been since the money was last taken out of the bank. Cash would then be taxed, so that the longer you "hoard" the money, the less it's worth.[6]

It appears that financial privacy is only going to continue to erode. When Sloan became director of FinCEN in April 1999, he assured *Money Laundering Alert* in an exclusive interview that he planned to " 'level the playing field.' We need to close loopholes. We don't want a leaky boat in our money laundering controls." He was referring to financial services that are not yet monitored the way banks are.[7] According to *Wired News*, "FinCEN hopes to expand its surveillance to include the insurance industry, pawn brokers and travel agents, and then use what it terms 'artificial intelligence' techniques to analyze the stream of data."[8]

If Sloan has his way, FinCEN is only the beginning of high-tech government surveillance.

Echelon

For years the government has used national security as a reason—and at times a rationalization—for granting extensive powers to federal agencies. These powers were needed in order to thwart the covert activities of international spies, but too often agencies used their vast resources to invade the privacy of ordinary citizens and trample underfoot their civil rights. As a result, in 1978 Congress passed the Foreign Intelligence Security Act. This act established the Foreign Intelligence Surveillance Court (FISC), an ultrasecret tribunal composed of seven federal district court judges. Theoretically, the purpose of this court was to establish accountability. Before intelligence agencies could set up wiretaps or search the homes of suspected spies, they had to obtain the court's approval. Practically, however, the court is little more than a rubber stamp; in its two-decade history it has rejected only one of the more than ten thousand requests submitted to it.[9]

Despite what Congress may have intended, no one is really policing government surveillance, and it continues to grow unabated. In fact, the U.S. government, along with Canada, Great

Britain, Australia, and New Zealand, today maintains a massive international spy system code-named "Echelon." Comprised of a vast network of satellites and listening stations around the world, Echelon intercepts and analyzes virtually every electronic transmission, worldwide. It has been suggested that the system intercepts as many as three billion communications every day, including phone calls, e-mail messages, Internet downloads, and fax transmissions.[10] Echelon's monitoring stations use advanced artificial intelligence systems to scan all communications and flag transmissions worthy of further investigation.

Though the National Security Administration (NSA) will neither confirm nor deny Echelon's existence, the governments of both Australia and New Zealand have acknowledged that the system is in place.[11] In addition, the European Parliament commissioned two reports that describe Echelon's activities. According to the American Civil Liberties Union (ACLU), "These reports unearthed a startling amount of evidence, which suggests that Echelon's powers may have been underestimated."[12]

Since that time, several major media stories—including those from *60 Minutes*,[13] the *New York Times*,[14] the *Washington Post*,[15] and the BBC[16]—have turned up a number of additional details. For one, the system has been used for corporate espionage. Patrick Poole, the former deputy director of the Center for Technology Policy at the Free Congress Foundation, outlined these in his excellent online white paper entitled "Echelon: America's Secret Global Surveillance Network."[17] According to his research,

President Clinton ordered the NSA and FBI to mount a massive surveillance operation at the 1993 Asian/Pacific Economic Conference (APEC) hosted in Seattle. One intelligence source ...

related that over 300 hotel rooms had been bugged for the event, which was designed to obtain information regarding oil and hydro-electric deals pending in Vietnam that were passed on to high level Democratic Party contributors competing for the contracts. But foreign companies were not the only losers: when Vietnam expressed interest in purchasing two used 737 freighter aircraft from an American businessman, the deal was scuttled after Commerce Secretary Ron Brown arranged favorable financing for two new 737s from Boeing.[18]

Moreover, Echelon has reportedly been used for domestic political purposes:

- In order to convince Richard Nixon to fire Secretary of State William P. Rogers, Henry Kissinger had the NSA intercept his messages, as Nixon aide John Ehrlichman revealed in his memoirs.
- Margaret Newsham, a former Lockheed software manager who was responsible for some of Echelon's computer systems, reported that she overheard a real-time interception of one of Senator Strom Thurmond's phone calls.
- Former Maryland congressman Michael Barnes claimed that during the Reagan administration his phone messages were routinely intercepted.
- In 1992 the *London Observer* revealed that the NSA had been monitoring Amnesty International, Greenpeace, and Christian Aid, a ministry that works in foreign countries with native pastors.[19]

These are only a few of the abuses that the NSA has perpetrated. Patrick Poole neatly summed up the situation:

It should hardly be surprising that Echelon ends up being used by elected and bureaucratic officials to their political advantage or by the intelligence agencies themselves for the purpose of sustaining their privileged surveillance powers and bloated budgets. The availability of such invasive technology practically begs for abuse, although it does not justify its use to those ends. But what is most frightening is the targeting of such "subversives" as those who expose corrupt government activity, protect human rights from government encroachments, challenge corporate polluters, or promote the gospel of Christ. That the vast intelligence powers of the United States should be arrayed against legitimate and peaceful organizations is demonstrative not of the desire to monitor, but of the desire to control.[20]

Carnivore

When EarthLink refused a court order demanding that the Internet service provider install the FBI's Carnivore program on its system, the FBI took the company to court.

EarthLink had two concerns. First, it feared that the FBI's e-mail surveillance software wouldn't be compatible with the company's operating system and would crash the system. Second, EarthLink executives complained that they had no way to confirm that Carnivore's use would be limited to finding the information that the FBI said it was looking for. In other words, EarthLink could not really guarantee the privacy it had promised its customers.

The federal magistrate ruled against EarthLink, so Carnivore was installed. As predicted, Carnivore was incompatible with the operating system, so the company had to install an older operating system that would allow Carnivore to do its job. The system crashed and a number of customers lost service.[21]

In the wake of the EarthLink conflict, *USA Today* reported:

> EarthLink spokesman Kurt Rahn said the company and
> FBI officials had agreed that EarthLink would collect such data
> in the future when investigators obtain a court order. "Basically,
> we reached a mutual agreement with the FBI that we would be
> able to monitor and gather the information that they needed
> ourselves," Rahn said. "That way, they got what they wanted
> and we were able to maintain the integrity of our network." [FBI
> spokesman Steven] Berry declined to confirm any such agree-
> ment or discuss at which Internet service providers the agency
> has installed Carnivore. Berry said the bureau is currently using
> the device, but he declined to say in how many cases or where.[22]

The FBI has insisted on using Carnivore despite a great deal
of understandable opposition from those who want to protect privacy. Basically, Carnivore is a computer system that sifts through
all e-mails coming from and going into an Internet service
provider. It scans the addresses of both sender and receiver, along
with the subject line, in order to decide whether to make a copy of
the entire message. Many privacy advocates fear that this system
has no limits, for it opens the e-mails of many people who are not
the subjects of investigations. Moreover, there is no accountability,
since only the FBI agents know what they are downloading from
the program. A traditional telephone wiretap, on the other hand,
targets calls *only* to and from the suspect, and is implemented by
the phone company.[23]

In response to criticism, Attorney General Janet Reno com-
missioned a supposedly independent review of the program.[24] The
FBI was supposed to keep the names of reviewers confidential.
Nevertheless, the bureau released a PDF document (a format for

exchanging documents digitally) with the names blacked out—even though anyone who had the PDF software could remove the black-outs easily.[25] Cyberjournalist Declan McCullagh wrote, "It's uncertain whether the irony of public disclosure of personal information, by the very people who are in the midst of claiming they can be trusted to protect it, was lost on Justice Department officials, because they declined to comment on Wednesday."[26]

WHOM CAN YOU TRUST?

Looking to government to protect our privacy is like looking to the fox to guard the henhouse. We can't expect Big Brother to stop watching us if we go to Big Brother for help. While we can and should all hope and work for a society that respects privacy, we cannot get there exclusively by trying to reform the government. We need to reform our own lives so that we don't give away our privacy.

It starts with us. The rest of this book is designed to help you take control of your own privacy. If more people would do this, much of the problem would go away.

PART TWO

DECIDE WHAT TO DO ABOUT IT

CHAPTER FIVE

MAKING THE DECISION AND SETTING GOALS

Chance fights ever on the side of the prudent.

—Euripides

M any people talk about the need for privacy. One of the first things they point to is just how few companies on the Internet actually follow their privacy policies. But what motivation is there for the companies to adhere to these policies? No one reads them. Consider that for every hundred thousand customers on Americangreetings.com, the Web's second largest retail site, only *nine* actually click on the site's privacy policy. That comes to less than a hundredth of a percentage point. Spokeswoman Nancy Davis stated, "It's so low it's barely statistically significant."[1]

But what of all the voiced concern, the proposed privacy legislation, and so on? That's perhaps a good start in addressing privacy issues, but ultimately it's not an accurate measure of how concerned most people are. You have to keep in mind the difference between the political demand for privacy and the economic demand. Economic demand is the more accurate measure of what people really want, as it reveals how much people are willing to sacrifice to reach a goal. In other words, how people spend their time and their money reveals their priorities.

Sure, people say they want privacy, but they're not doing much to secure it. If virtually no one reads privacy statements in the first place, it makes little difference that Bloomingdales.com, LLBean.com, Ticketmaster Online, and many others openly acknowledge that they give out customer data to their partners.[2] Customers continue to shop at these sites, unaffected by how these companies are actively compromising their privacy.

What about you?

You are going to have to make a decision: *what are you willing to do to protect your privacy?* Corporations will not be willing to give up the asset of their customer database when so few people even care about privacy statements. Political groundswells are not going to be able to overcome credit agencies, corporations, and other lobbying groups when politicians realize how little people actually care about their privacy. You are going to have to decide if you really want to protect your own privacy. No one is going to do for you what you are unwilling to do for yourself.

STARTING WITH ONE

Fortunately, if you truly want your privacy, you can have it.

I wrote this book both to persuade you that the end of privacy is a serious issue and to inform you about how you can maintain your privacy despite what is happening in our country. Ultimately, the best and most productive way to counter the larger movement toward the end of privacy is to take back your own privacy.

If you begin to take your privacy seriously and take steps to protect it, then you might find that others will do the same. At first you will have an impact on your circle of friends. People will want to know why you use an anonymous browser or remailer, or why you use a drop box rather than your street address. Relatives will want to know why you protect your Social Security number. Because you demonstrate real concern for privacy in the way you live, you will be more persuasive when you talk about such issues with others. Ideas have consequences *only* when acted upon.

You may have even broader impact. If more and more people take steps to protect their own privacy, then politicians and businesses will find that they have to pay attention. More people pursuing privacy will mean that companies will find it more difficult to track them. They will have to come up with believable privacy policies in order to connect with consumers. Firms developing and selling products to protect privacy will grow larger, and, as they expand, they will spread the concern for privacy through their advertising. Eventually politicians and bureaucrats may respond with decent rules to protect privacy and may think twice about intrusive measures.

If even a minority of the population demonstrates an economic desire for privacy, that may well change things considerably in the business world and give the government incentive to change as well. But if all we do is talk about it, then we can expect the erosion of our privacy to continue unabated.

It is up to you. Before you can make any progress in reclaiming your privacy, you must believe that privacy is worth preserving. Let me warn you: privacy is not always convenient, easy, or cheap, but you must be willing to pay the price to secure it.

PAYING THE PRICE

Jack and Melinda Kelley[3] had all but given up trying to have a baby. So they were quite joyfully surprised when Melinda got pregnant. The only problem was that Jack had recently quit his job and relocated his family to go to school. As a full-time student, caught without insurance for the pregnancy, he had no idea how he could afford to remain in school with the medical expenses that were involved.

Fortunately, the couple learned that a local Catholic hospital would give free or reduced services to needy families. They applied for aid and found that the hospital first wanted them to apply for Medicaid. Though they hadn't originally intended to use government services, they went ahead and applied for the aid. The pregnancy and delivery went fine, and Melinda learned that once the baby was born they would be eligible for more free services. They could get food or formula that would save hundreds of dollars each month.

But in the end they decided they were better off surviving on their own.

It was not that they felt guilty about taking government handouts. In order to make ends meet, Jack was still working as well as going to school. This was simply a temporary situation in which they could use the government's help.

But, as they soon discovered, government assistance wasn't really free after all. In their estimation, the cost of "free" food and assistance was too high.

It cost them their privacy.

Melinda found that she was under the scrutiny of government employees every time she went in to get her vouchers. They would ask her nosy questions about her child-rearing methods. She felt this was none of their business. They would lecture her on subjects that she already knew about. She did not like being under their surveillance and being evaluated according to their rather debatable standards of good child care—standards that she felt pressured to accept. Finally, she told Jack she couldn't take it anymore. Jack agreed.

In making their decision, Jack and Melinda came face to face with the fact that recovering privacy often means losing benefits. For Jack it meant working more hours and having a more difficult time as a student. But it was more than worth the sacrifice as far as they were concerned.

Though your situation is probably quite different from Jack and Melinda's, what they learned is just as real for you as it was for them. Privacy isn't free. It means spending time and money while sacrificing some convenience.

DECIDING WHAT TO DO

While privacy is certainly a growing concern for a number of people, not everyone has the same specific prescription for the problem or even the same sense of what should be kept private. Consider the various groups involved in lobbying for privacy. The ACLU is a liberal organization that often calls on the government to enact reforms. Privacilla and the Cato Institute are libertarian groups that want businesses unregulated beyond meeting their contractual obligations, believing that government needs to be restrained. Other groups have more specific concerns. For instance, organizations such as CASPIAN (Consumers Against Supermarket Privacy Invasion and Numbering) and No Cards! attempt to pressure retailers to halt their card savings programs, saying these violate privacy and are probably fraudulent, since one can't be sure if cardholders really save money or if noncardholders are being penalized for withholding personal information.

And not all individuals pursue privacy in the same way. In other words, people have different goals when it comes to privacy. Some are concerned only about their personal information being bought and sold by companies. Others are concerned about identity theft, lawsuits, and what may happen if their personal information gets in the wrong hands. Still others are concerned about an increasingly lawless government and what can happen when innocent citizens become targets.

In short, you must decide for yourself what your privacy goals are. I can't tell you exactly what you should do to preserve your privacy because it depends on what *sort* of privacy you want. What I can do is give you a framework for making an informed decision. What kind of privacy do you want? What kind of privacy do you need? What kind of privacy can you afford? These are the questions you need to ask yourself.

Counting the Cost

Different sorts of privacy demand different levels of sacrifice and effort. You must set realistic goals for yourself according to your beliefs and desires.[4]

Before you can begin to recover your privacy, you need to set yourself attainable goals that are appropriate to who you are, what you have, and what you want. You need to sit down and think about what you are trying to accomplish and seriously consider what it will take to do so. This is important because privacy is *not* an all-or-nothing proposition.

Which Privacy?

Much of what we're talking about is *risk management*. You have to determine the degree of privacy you are after as well as how much time, energy, and money you are willing to spend in order to attain that privacy.

Personally, I wish everyone would acquire as much privacy as he or she possibly can. The threats to privacy are growing, and I want to see these trends reversed. But not everyone can do everything all at once. If I were simply to tell people that they must deal with *all* privacy concerns at once, then many people, feeling overwhelmed, would do nothing at all.

What I want you to understand is that even if you can't do everything to secure more privacy for yourself, you can do something. Doing something is always better than nothing. You will be reducing your risk of victimization, and you will be adding to what I believe is a growing movement to reclaim our collective privacy.

THREE-DIMENSIONAL PRIVACY

To help you evaluate what you are willing to do and how much it will cost to get what you want, I have developed a way to think about privacy that breaks it into different levels of commitment, expense, and realized privacy. I call this concept "three-dimensional privacy." This model will allow you to determine your own privacy goals based on your lifestyle, financial resources, and personal values.

The First Dimension

The first level offers simple protection from the threat posed by commercial enterprises, including bankers, insurance companies, and health-care providers, who want to sell or use your private information to exploit you. It is the easiest level of privacy to attain. It doesn't take much money—just a little effort and discipline.

The main requirement is to develop new habits. As we will see in the next chapter, your own actions—or inactions, more often—are responsible for claiming a great deal of your privacy. We live in a society that expects us to give away our privacy and that rewards us for doing so. You will have to *think* about the ways you act or the things you passively allow to take place, and you will have to *discipline* yourself to behave differently.

You will also need to be willing to spend a little time. Taking the time to learn about privacy issues is a necessary first step—one you're already taking by reading this book. But you will also need to take the time to read companies' privacy policies, find out which have "opt-out" programs in place, and place the appropriate phone calls to make your identity a little less open to those who might be searching for a target. Most importantly, you will have to learn the art of saying no to nosy organizations that ask for information that is none of their business. At first, this may make you uncomfortable, but over time—and with practice—it will get easier.

The Second Dimension

Building on Dimension One, this level offers protection from the threat posed by attorneys, hackers, and outright criminals who want to use your private information to *harm* you. This takes a little more work and expense, but it is attainable for those who want it.

When you think about this level of privacy you need to ask yourself what might happen if you became the victim of credit card fraud or identity theft. What if a spurious and malicious lawsuit were brought against you? What if you were to lose everything you have worked so hard for? In answering these sorts of questions, you will determine to what extent you want Dimension Two privacy.

The Third Dimension

This level offers protection from the threat posed by federal, state, and local governments who want to gain access to your private information. With new technologies, the government, too, can assemble massive databases with our private information. The most recent U.S. Census, for example, made it clear the federal government is doing just that.

Some citizens received census forms that asked for their Social Security number, as Kenneth Prewitt, director of the U.S. Census Bureau, acknowledged in testimony before Congress.[5] The Census Bureau can use the Social Security number to request information from other government agencies and combine it with their own. Indeed, Prewitt told Congress: "Section 6 of Title 13, United States Code, specifically authorizes the Census Bureau to acquire data from other agencies instead of conducting direct inquiries. The Social Security numbers collected in these surveys permit us to combine survey responses with their corresponding administrative data for program evaluation and enhancement."[6] In other words, the government is making a concerted effort to consolidate data collected by various agencies. Prewitt stated that the aim of this data collection was the "enhancement" of government programs, but some might find it disconcerting that the government can build a master database on its citizens.

Because governments have such vast resources at their disposal, it is difficult to evade their intrusions into our private lives—it can take a considerable investment of time and energy. But the loss of our privacy and freedom will only become more pervasive unless you and I begin resisting their efforts. You will need to decide if and when you want to implement a strategy to avoid this sort of scrutiny. While protecting yourself from government intrusions is the most expensive form of privacy, I can show you the least expensive way to attain it.

No Absolute Privacy

No matter what precautions you take, securing *absolute privacy* is impossible. Anyone with enough time, money, and commitment will eventually find you and learn everything he wants to know. But the good news is that you don't need absolute privacy. *Essential privacy* will suffice. It's a bit like protecting your home and family. Personally, I believe strongly in the concept of self-defense, and I think it is prudent to take action to protect my family. Still, I realize that, even if I were to turn my house into a fortress, I couldn't achieve absolute protection. Someone with enough time and money who is dead set on penetrating my home defense system will do so. But I need only *essential* protection. I have a fence, dogs, an alarm system, and guns to protect my family from all but the truly committed. Basically, I want to be a difficult target. I want anyone who considers invading my home to think, *You know, this is gonna be a lot of work. I might even get hurt. I think I'll move on to someone who is a little less protected.*

The same is true when it comes to privacy. Your primary goal should be to make it difficult for all but the truly committed.

NO MAN IS AN ISLAND

Whatever you decide regarding your immediate and long-term goals for privacy, you are going to need help in implementing the decision. Those who know your street address will have to be told to send mail to a drop box. Those who know your primary e-mail address will need to know you don't want it given out to others. You will have to let people know if you get an unlisted phone number.

You will, of course, have to work with members of your immediate family even more closely in making your privacy decisions. Without their support, involvement, and input into what goals you should pursue, your attempt to take back your privacy will never get off the ground. You need to make sure they are all on board with you in this endeavor. After all, they know everything about you, and you about them. Their privacy is your privacy and vice versa. You need to work together.

GETTING YOUR HOUSE IN ORDER

A key benefit of trying to recover your privacy is that it will force you into habits of self-reliance.

One of the reasons I became concerned about the end of privacy, and with informing others about it, was that I have been practicing and promoting self-reliant living. I define self-reliance as *the ability to maintain one's freedom, safety, and comfort with minimal dependence on external institutions or infrastructures*. In other words, it is the willingness to take responsibility for one's own life. I encourage people to plan ahead, decrease their dependence on others, and make decisions that will allow them to function without being vulnerable.

Pursuing privacy is an important first step in doing this, for it will likely motivate you to take other actions, such as getting out of debt and preparing for emergencies. For example, if your finances are in a state of disarray, you may be intimidated by what it takes to achieve Dimension Three privacy. After all, you will need to make privacy decisions based on an accurate assessment of your budget. But you can start small and pursue Dimension One privacy first. That, in turn, could convince you to work on getting out of debt, saving some money, and then moving on to Dimensions Two and Three.

Ultimately, self-reliance puts us in a better position to serve *others*, and privacy is a vital part of this. By reclaiming your privacy and becoming self-reliant, you will be in a position to help someone who is victimized due to his lack of privacy. If you know someone who is being stalked or defrauded through identity theft, for instance, you will have the knowledge from personal experience to help that person protect himself. Moreover, if you are self-reliant, you can provide for your own needs and the needs of those under your care. In a crisis or economic downturn, you will be one less person for whom someone else—including the government—has to provide. And that way, you and others won't have to suffer the intrusions and scrutiny that so often come with depending on government services.

GET TO WORK

The end of privacy is really just part of the end of freedom. Whether professional or amateur criminals, brutally impersonal corporations, or intrusive state and federal government agencies, there are forces at work taking away your privacy for their own gain. Dealing with these forces and taking back your privacy will demand some effort. But freedom always comes at a price. The problem is that people today are too often willing to surrender their freedom as soon as maintaining it becomes inconvenient.

You must resist the temptation to give in so easily. With a little time and effort, you can and will regain your privacy. And I will show you the procedures and discipline to reach your goals.

PRACTICAL PRIVACY TIP #6:
Think About Everyday Privacy Threats

As you begin to determine what sort of privacy you want to achieve, you should think about how you might be compromising your privacy in your everyday life. One way to do this is to take the privacy self-assessment found in Appendix A. But there are other threats to your privacy you might not even think about. In an excellent special report for the *New York Times*, Nina Bernstein showed readers how the typical consumer sacrifices his privacy each and every day.[7] Think about what happens to you when you do the following:

1. **Get a prescription filled.** Once you fill a prescription, the pharmacy has your name linked to the drug in its database. As noted in the Introduction, pharmacy chains such as Rite Aid have used information from their databases for targeted marketing or sold it to other marketers. As a result, you could end up being bombarded with sales pitches.

2   **Call a toll-free number.** If you call an 800 number, it will automatically capture your phone number (even if it's unlisted). Armed with your phone number, marketers can easily pull up your name and address. Once you are on its list, the company can use your information for its own purposes or sell your profile to other marketers.

3. **Use a supermarket discount card.** When you pay with a discount card, the supermarket has a record of every single item you purchase. Using sophisticated data-mining procedures, the store can create a profile of your buying habits and target you with other discount offers.

4. **Order from a catalog.** When you buy items from a mail-order catalog, the company you order from puts you on its list. You

will obviously continue to receive catalogs from that company, and it will also target you with offers tailored to your interests (determined by the type of merchandise you bought). If you pay with a credit card, your credit card company could also put you on a list based on the item you purchased.

CHAPTER SIX

PROCEDURES AND DISCIPLINE

In preparing for battle I have always found that plans are useless, but planning is indispensable.

—Dwight D. Eisenhower

The General Electric Company wanted to learn about the thinking of its thousands of investors. So it sent them a survey. The cover letter explained that "GE Investments is committed to providing superior quality service to you as a member of our core group of investors. To achieve this goal, we must clearly understand what is most important to you and how well your expectations are being met. Your feedback is necessary to make certain we have a clear picture of how we can best serve you."[1]

This survey was strictly anonymous—and for good reason. It asked quite personal questions, such as, "What percentage of your total investments are managed by GE Investments?" Anyone answering that GE managed the vast majority of his investments would be letting the company know that it had most of his private financial information at its disposal. Obviously, people would not want to answer that question if their identities could be known. The survey also requested that participants select a depiction that would "best describe their current investment needs."[2] Again, this is hardly the kind of information an investor would want his investment company to know about him.

The only problem was that the survey was *not* truly anonymous. Even though GE was asking for private information and even though respondents expected anonymity, the company wanted to know who filled out each form. The manager of GE Investments shareholder communications, Barbara Liedeker, wrote a letter to the company that had printed GE's survey, complimenting one employee in particular: "The hard part came with our request to 'secretly' identify each respondent in a most discrete [*sic*] way. I must especially compliment one of your employees,... who came up with an excellent solution to this problem. Her suggestion enabled us to secrete the code in a manner least likely to attract attention from the respondent. She's terrific!"[3]

Privacytimes.com got hold of this letter and showed that GE was actually tracking which investor said what. Each survey had an individualized number on it that looked like a standard direct mail source code. Liedeker wrote, "Our intention was to be able to, if we chose to, connect the particular completed questionnaire with the specific shareholder who filled it out, to get a profile of the share-holder."[4] She described how GE Investments wanted to identify responses to the survey that the company deemed to require "action": "We wanted to look at the nature of the account. [Were we] talking about an account worth a thousand dollars or an account worth a million dollars? Were we talking about an account that was recently established or one that was ten years old? Were we talking to a GE employee or a non-employee? We needed to know, based on the answers to the questions ... the source, which was the account shareholder who filled out the application.... And yet we wanted them to feel, when they were filling it out, that it was anonymous."[5]

Apparently, this sort of betrayal of trust is perfectly legal. Companies may suffer from a bad reputation if they get caught, but that's all. GE Investments and other companies could have surreptitiously tracked respondents to surveys many times before and simply never been caught. Of course, Tim Benedict, the company spokesman, claimed this was the first and only time that GE had done or would do such a thing.[6] But according to Jason Catlett, the president of Junkbusters Corporation, "Those sort of tricks are quite common in the survey industry. There's an assumption that reasonable people have that because their name does not appear they're anonymous.... In any survey, you should assume your response is not anonymous."[7]

To add insult to injury, GE's privacy policy, on its Financial Assurance Web site, reads:

> The General Electric Company, GE, is sensitive to privacy issues on the Internet. We believe it is important you know how we treat the information about you we receive on the Internet. In general, you can visit GE on the World Wide Web without telling us who you are or revealing any information about yourself. When information is needed, we will try to let you know at the time of collection how we will use the personal information.... At times we conduct on-line surveys to better understand the needs and profile of our visitors. When we conduct a survey, we will try to let you know how we will use the information at the time we collect information from you on the Internet.[8]

While this survey was done through the postal service, not over the Internet, it is nevertheless a gross display of hypocrisy for a company to acknowledge such privacy concerns and then to devise a plan to invade its investors' privacy. The doublespeak the company spokesman employed to explain GE's actions was equally cynical: "We basically didn't ask for the customer's name and address because we wanted to encourage a response. We wanted to know who was answering…. It was not to pull a fast one on our customers."[9]

These are the ways businesses can track us if we let them. But there are worse threats to our privacy than a deceptive survey. As bad as it is that we can be fooled into giving away our privacy, it is much worse that we can be persuaded to give it away *willingly*.

Contrary to what most people think, their biggest enemy is not big business and industry. It is not unscrupulous lawyers or criminals, or even the federal government. The biggest enemy to your privacy is *your own big mouth*.

Day in and day out, many of us fork over private information to anyone who asks. Whether it's a retail clerk, a telephone solicitor, a census worker, or even a public school official, we volunteer information that is essential to our privacy and freedom. As a result we are harassed by telemarketers and junk mail. Worse, we run a great risk of being exploited by criminals who get our personal information.

But you can counter this threat through clearly established procedures, cooperation from your family and friends, and the discipline to implement your plan.

AVOIDING THE WRONG STRATEGY

Before you begin developing the proper procedures and habits that are essential to protecting your privacy, you must be aware of certain habits you do not want to fall into. Do not act overtly secretive or paranoid, since you will only end up drawing attention to yourself. Your goal should be for no one to realize that you are trying to protect your privacy except those whom you choose to tell about it. Getting people to notice your privacy means you are *jeopardizing* your privacy.

When someone asks for information you do not think he has a right to, you need to be firm but polite. Don't say simply, "I'm not going to tell you that!" but rather, "I'm sorry, but we have a policy against giving out that kind of information." Even though it is your right to withhold information, it is wise to be ready with an explanation that will keep someone from becoming hostile or suspicious. If pressed, you might say, "You may not realize this, but identity theft is one of the fastest growing crimes in this country. Giving out personal information is extremely risky. I've made it my goal not to become a victim by giving out details about my life."

Whatever you do, be confident and firm. Don't act as if you have something to hide. It's amazing how fast those asking will back down.

FIRST STRATEGY: SILENCE IS GOLDEN

Agree with your family members that you will never, under any circumstances, give out your private information. In the chapters ahead, I will show you exactly how to do this, but for now you must make a raw commitment. You must be willing to forgo discounts, convenience, and other privileges if necessary. You will be amazed at how often you are asked for confidential, personal information.

Your first line of defense is simply to refuse to give out personal information. As John Boyle O'Reilly wrote in *Rules of the Road*, "Be silent and safe—silence never betrays you."[10] Recently, I wanted to sign up for a high-speed, broadband computer line. When I called one of the companies to place my order, the first thing the company representative asked me for after my name was my Social Security number. I went through the routine I suggested above—"I'm sorry, but I have a policy...."

The phone rep replied, "Well, sir, I must have your Social Security number to open an account."

At that point I said, "Well, if that's the case, then I'm afraid I'll have to take my business to a company that's not quite so nosy!"

I was about to hang up when he said, "Please hold while I check with my supervisor." Click. Muzak.

Fifteen seconds later he came back on the line. "No problem. What's the address where you want the service installed?" He continued to set up the account as though the initial exchange had never happened. Sometimes you just have to be assertive.

If a company representative is particularly insistent on receiving your personal information, you can make him think twice about what he is requesting by asking:

- "Why do you need this information?"
- "Where will you store the information?"
- "How long will you keep the information?"
- "What systems do you have in place to protect my information?"
- "What recourse will I have if this information falls into other hands?"

And if you ask for such explanations in writing, you give the company a chance to rethink its policy. Perhaps it will see the light. If not, at least you will have made an impact. If more and more people keep asking such questions and then refuse to give the information, the company may decide it would rather sell a product than simply enforce its policy of information acquisition.

PRACTICAL PRIVACY TIP #7:
What to Do If Someone Demands Your Social Security Number

In his very helpful article "What to Do When They Ask for Your Social Security Number,"[12] Chris Hibbert, a privacy activist with the Computer Professionals for Social Responsibility, suggests seven strategies:

1. **Talk to people higher up in the organization.** This often works simply because the organization has a standard way of dealing with requests not to use the SSN, and the first person you deal with just hasn't been around long enough to know what it is.

2. **Enlist the aid of your employer.** Personnel and benefits departments often carry a lot of weight when dealing with health insurance companies. You have to decide whether talking to someone in personnel and possibly trying to change corporate policy is going to get back to your supervisor and affect your job.

3. **Threaten to complain to a consumer affairs bureau.** You can call most newspapers and ask for their "Action Line" or equivalent. If you're dealing with a local government agency, look in the state or local government section of the phone book under "consumer affairs." If it's a federal agency, your congressional representative may be able to help.

4. **Insist that the organization document a corporate policy requiring the number.** When someone can't find a written policy or doesn't want to push hard enough to get it, he'll often realize that he doesn't know what the policy is and has just been following routine.

5. **Ask what the organization needs it for and suggest alternatives.** If you're talking to someone who has some independence

and is willing to help, he will sometimes reveal why the company wants it, and then you can satisfy that requirement in a
different way.

6. **Tell the organization you'll take your business elsewhere.**
    Follow through on this promise if the company doesn't cooper-
    ate.

7. **Be especially reluctant to give up your SSN if you've already
    gotten service.** If someone insists you have to provide your
    number in order to continue the relationship, you can choose to
    ignore the request in hopes that the organization will forget or
    find another solution before you get tired of the interruption.

It is not just on the phone that you must be vigilant. Usually
when you order products or services online, register a product, or
fill out a warranty, you are given the opportunity to fill in a lot of
information about yourself. Many times the required information
is quite minimal and is marked in some way—often by an asterisk
near the mandatory blanks. You should make it your habit never to
provide more information than necessary.

Remember, even if it is okay to give a specific company a certain amount of information—even if you trust the company not to
share the data, not to use it to manipulate you, and not to store it in
an unsafe place—you are still developing bad habits by giving away
personal information. Besides, you never know when the company
will change management, policy, or both. You are much better off
being in the *habit* of not giving out information about yourself.[11]

SECOND STRATEGY: PUTTING UP A FRONT

Unfortunately, we often *must* provide certain information in
order to buy goods and services. In these cases, the first strategy

won't suffice. Still, there are ways to protect your *real* information by establishing a secondary layer of legitimate data (sometimes called a "ghost identity") intended for public consumption. This is perfectly legal, and it allows you to protect your most sensitive personal information while still getting the products you need and want.

If refusing to give information fails, fall back on this second line of defense. If the company insists it needs your personal information, give your "public" information. I have never had a company or government agency press beyond this—even when I'm applying for a credit card, opening a bank account, or securing a driver's license.

You can create this secondary layer of information by doing several things. To start with, consider acquiring a secondary voice-mail box, getting a post office box or a mail drop, getting a Web-based e-mail address, and perhaps even establishing an alias.

Get a Secondary Voice-Mail Box

For less than $15 a month, you can get a voice-mail-only phone number. The number doesn't ring anywhere. When people call this number, they will receive a voice-mail message that you record. They will simply think you are out or on another call. You can pick up these messages just as you would with any other voice-mail box.

Give this "public" number out to everyone who is not part of your family or a close personal friend. That way you will never have to listen to telemarketing calls in the middle of dinner.

Get a Personal Mail Drop

A post office box will keep your physical address unknown. A mail drop address, such as those provided by Mailboxes Etc., will allow you to receive UPS shipments. This will cost you $10 to $20 a month, but it is well worth it. It will provide you with not simply an alternative place to receive mail but an alternative that *looks* like a street address.

When you obtain a mail drop, the company will require you to fill out United States Postal Service Form 1583: Application for Delivery of Mail Through Agent.[13] When submitting the form, you have to provide two forms of identification. Acceptable identification includes: valid driver's license or state nondriver's identification card; armed forces, government, university, or recognized corporate identification card; passport or alien registration card or certificate of naturalization; current lease, mortgage, or deed of trust; voter or vehicle registration card; and home or vehicle insurance policy. The agent may retain a photocopy of your identification for verification.[14]

One potential problem is that Postal Service Form 1583 requires you to provide your "home address." You basically have three options here:

1. *Provide your real address.* The problem with this is that you can't control how the mail drop company protects this information. What if a criminal or private investigator uses a believable pretext to get your information? It's not that difficult, and it's been done before.

2. *Provide your soon-to-be-previous address.* Before your move, go in and apply for a mail box. If it's in another city, tell the company you are working in the area and need a mail box to receive local mail while you are on assignment. (Bear in mind that Form 1583 says you must update the information—including your home address—whenever it changes, but, well, you may decide to forget this.)

3. *Provide another mail drop address.* Technically this isn't your home address, of course, so it's up to you to decide whether

you want to take this approach. But if you elect to use it, be advised that most mail drops are aware of other mail drop addresses in the same city. You will also need to make sure the first mail drop address—the one you are representing as your home address—is listed on your driver's license and other ID.

You may want to look into a privately owned, local mail-drop company. These companies tend to be a little more flexible, and they are also less likely to give out your real address to a private investigator or criminal with a plausible pretext.

Once you have secured a mail drop, give the address out whenever anyone asks for your home address. Do not receive any mail—none!—at your home address. In fact, if you have been receiving mail at your home, file a change of address at the post office and have all mail forwarded to your new drop. For more details on mail privacy, see Chapter 9.

Get a Web-based E-mail Address

This is your "public" address for the Internet. Use it whenever you are required to give out an e-mail address in order to complete a transaction, and give it out to anyone who is not family or a personal friend. Inevitably, this address will be overwhelmed with spam. When it gets unbearable, simply change addresses.

Such Web-based addresses include Hotmail.com, Yahoo.com, and Netzero.com. To see all the options, you can visit Emailaddresses.com, which has an international listing and reviews of all the available Web-based e-mail addresses.[16] The owners of the site constantly update the list itself as well as the reviews.

Some of these free addresses are quite anonymous. For example, Hotmail does not even require another e-mail address. For

PRACTICAL PRIVACY TIP #8:
Understand the Advantages of a Private Mailbox Over a P.O. Box

ACL Security, a company in Finland, has produced a list of advantages to using a mail-forwarding company rather than simply a post office box:[15]

1. Arranging a mail drop is usually much simpler than setting up a post office box. With the former you simply pay your money and gain immediate access, whereas with the latter there are usually delays.

2. With a mail drop you usually have an actual street address. As a result, others assume it is your private residence.

3. You can always check your mail or give specific instructions, such as mail forwarding, by phone, fax, or letter. With a post office box you are on your own.

4. A mail drop will accept courier services such as UPS or FedEx; a post office box won't.

5. A private mail drop protects your privacy much more effectively. It is relatively easy to get a customer's street address from a post office.

6. The post office will demand to know the details of your identity, whereas you usually can engage the services of a mail drop with much greater privacy.

7. A mail drop is usually able to receive a letter in an outer envelope from you and mail the inner envelope from that location, giving you more confidentiality.

8. A mail drop generally gives you a host of other services as well, including photocopying, faxing, and word processing.

9. A mail drop can also function as a way of keeping valuables safe away from your own residence.

those that do, you can always open up an anonymous Hotmail account in order to give the other account somewhere to send its welcome message. In signing up for these services, you do *not* need to provide a current address.

Why do you need such an e-mail address? Just to mention a few things:

- Some companies require an e-mail address before they will let you download their "free" product. Once they get your e-mail address, many of them will begin sending you e-mail or, worse, will sell your address to other companies.
- Whenever you want to participate in an open newsgroup or discussion group, you must register with an e-mail address. You don't know what sorts of people may end up reading your post, so you need to be protected. In addition, there are programs that do nothing but comb newsgroups, "harvesting" e-mail addresses for professional spammers (a.k.a. "bulk e-mail marketers").
- If ordering online, you need to provide an e-mail address that will keep your primary address from getting sold to other companies.

Establish an Alias

Once you have an alternative physical address, an alternative e-mail address, and an alternative phone number, it is easy to take the next step and produce an alternative name to put between yourself and those who would pry into your private life. Use this name whenever you are asked for information and don't want to reveal your true identity. You can even establish an alias e-mail address. In fact, this is probably the easiest way to establish an alternative identity.

PRACTICAL PRIVACY TIP #9:
Five Reasons to Get a Secondary, Free E-mail Account

Emailaddresses.com points out four advantages to having a free, Web-based e-mail account.[17] I have added a fifth:

1. **E-mail from work.** If your employer monitors or blocks your e-mail but you have Web access, Web-based e-mail enables you to communicate with family and friends without having to rely on the telephone.

2. **Anonymity.** Obviously, this is the main reason why I am recommending this sort of e-mail address. Emailaddresses.com points out that there are support groups on the Web, such as Alcoholics Anonymous, for which one might need additional privacy.

3. **Primary e-mail address as a hotline.** If you use your primary e-mail only for a select few close friends and family, then your inbox won't be overflowing with junk e-mail, which might make you miss the important stuff.

4. **Freedom from spam.** If you use an e-mail address in promoting a Web page you've developed (or anything else), you will find you get torrents of spam. A throwaway Web-based e-mail address will take care of this problem.

5. **Privacy at home.** This fifth point is my own. You might also need privacy while you're at home. If you are counseling someone with a personal problem, for example, you might want to give him or her a way to reach you that your children can't read.

One of the advantages of an alternative identity is that you can use a different one for each different activity. That way, when you get junk mail sent to your drop box, you will be able to tell who shared your personal information with others. For example, a preapproved credit card that arrives for a name under which you recently subscribed to a magazine will tell you that the magazine shared your information.

I suggest using the most common name you can think of—"Smith," "Jones," "White." This makes it that much more difficult to track the name back to you. Don't use something unique and memorable. Save your creativity for some other project.

If you decide to be serious about constructing a makeshift identity, you are going to have to put some work into keeping track of your alter ego. Some forms of alternative identity might not require much foresight or planning—such as surveys from nosy businesses in which you simply want to be as wildly unconventional as possible. In other cases, more caution and careful record keeping will be necessary. You will need to make sure your mail-drop service knows that your alias will also be receiving mail at this address. You will need to write down which name is associated with which Web-based e-mail address, as well as the attendant password. Make sure your alternative identities are consistent and don't get confused with one another.

THIRD STRATEGY: RETREAT AND REGROUP

Finally, if necessary, you have to be willing to take your business elsewhere or even deprive yourself of the service. This will happen, and it will be painful, but it might not last. If enough people do this, companies will eventually get the message. Unfortunately, not enough people are presently doing it, so companies persist in their intrusive collection of personal data. So, in the meantime, we are going to have to put up with certain losses. Even when you are armed with explanations for why you will not give out your personal information, some companies will not back down. Count on it.

Remember, privacy is inconvenient and at times expensive. Still, your refusal to give information now can have positive effects in the future. Neither companies nor government agencies will get the message unless they meet with resistance. Resistance now simply means doing without a few conveniences. If the forces at work continue to erode our privacy, we might find that giving away the details of our lives is no longer considered a matter of voluntary cooperation. It's time to draw the line!

In the chapters that follow, we will employ even more detailed strategies.

PART THREE

EMPLOY APPROPRIATE COUNTERMEASURES

CHAPTER SEVEN

COMPUTERS AND THE INTERNET

What will you do when cyberspace becomes a kind of Orwellian Cheers bar, where everyone knows your name, even the people you don't want to? And not only your name, but where you went last night, what you had for breakfast, and a thousand other little factoids about you.

—Jason Catlett, president of Junkbusters

Mention the word "privacy" and most people immediately think of their computer and the Internet. The Internet offers enormous potential for freedom. Some even argue that the vast proliferation of information the Internet allows will ultimately make it impossible for totalitarian regimes to survive. Regardless, widespread use of the Internet makes it possible for us to be tracked and controlled as never before.

Every Web site you visit—every keystroke you make—can be tracked. In fact, current technology enables an outsider to invade your computer without your knowledge and suck the files off your hard drive.

Every time you log on to the Web, your Internet service provider assigns you a unique electronic identity. This identity is then used to log every Web site you visit, every e-mail you send, and every newsgroup you post to. Worse, these logs are archived, so that anyone with the initiative and the know-how can profile your interests and concerns.

FIRST DIMENSION STRATEGIES

There are some ways you can protect your privacy from those who wish to track you on the Web for commercial purposes. In this chapter I'm going to recommend several specific products.* But bear in mind that technology is progressing rapidly, so by the time you're reading this some of my recommendations may no longer be available or better solutions may have come along. For an up-to-date list of my recommendations, visit my Web site at www.moreprivacy.com.

Cookies

"Cookies" are little text files slipped to your Web browser. When you visit a site, these cookies mark you so that the site will recognize you the next time you surf to that Web page. This is how some Web sites like Amazon.com can greet you by name when you log on. Cookies come not only from the site you're on but also from another site that has bought a banner ad on the site you're visiting. In general, banner ads are more insidious because the same company will have ads on several sites and will attempt to profile you as it tracks you from one Web page to another. DoubleClick is the best known of the banner ad companies.

---

* Note: The products I recommend are designed for the Windows platform. Since Macs represent only about 8 percent of the personal computer market, not many software developers write software for this platform.

Cookies don't usually identify you by name but only mark you and then keep track of when you visit their Web sites. However, if you order something online, fill out a survey, or give away your information for some other reason, the cookies can then link your identity with your movement.

How do you deal with this? Simple. Browsers have the option of turning off cookies. Different browsers do it slightly differently, but you want to look for "preferences." On Netscape you can choose to block all cookies or just those coming from a source other than the Web site. On Internet Explorer you can have session cookies that allow the sites to recognize you while you are browsing but that are deleted when you close the browser. I personally have persistent cookies turned off and session cookies turned on.

Be forewarned: some sites will not allow you to visit when you turn cookies off, or some features may not be available. Oh well, that's just part of the price you pay for privacy. As I've said, privacy isn't always convenient.

Proxy Servers

Proxy servers are Web sites that act as an intermediary between a Web page and your computer, giving you even more protection. Some of these are free services and others require a subscription. You will find a collection of links to some of these proxy servers at Privacy.net under third-party proxies.[1]

When using these servers, you can leave your cookies alone, but you do need to turn off your Java scripts because pop-up windows can sometimes establish links directly to your computer without the proxy. In that case you are no longer anonymous to whoever sent the pop-up window.

ActiveX

If you are browsing with Internet Explorer, you need to disable your ActiveX plug-ins, which run through your browser. Even with a third-party proxy, you can be identified with these programs. In fact, ActiveX can damage your computer and violate your privacy.

ActiveX is essentially a Windows program that runs whenever your browser encounters it on a Web page. It can do virtually anything a Windows program can do. It is not a virus, so scanning is useless. It is not a download, so you do not have to open it—it opens as soon as you allow it on your browser. Your browser will warn you against "unsigned" ActiveX controls, but there is no real reason a hacker couldn't get a signature under false pretenses. A critic of Microsoft actually developed an ActiveX control that shut down the computer in order to demonstrate how powerful ActiveX controls should be.[2]

For specific instructions on how to disable ActiveX, see Practical Privacy Tip #10.

Filtering Ads

Advertisements or "banners" on the Web work only if they are distracting. As a result, banner ads often are eyesores, and many times you have to wait for the flashing banner to download. But worst of all, banners track you with cookies profiling your online surfing and purchasing habits.

To block these banners you can use a third-party proxy service designed specifically for that purpose. Internet Junkbuster Proxy and Guidescope are both free and will do the job. See the Junkbusters Web page (www.junkbusters.com/ht/en/guidescope.html) to choose which proxy service will work best for you. I personally use Guidescope and love it.

PRACTICAL PRIVACY TIP #10:
Set Up Internet Explorer for *Functional* Privacy

I use Internet Explorer and have customized my security prefer-ences. You could simply choose "High" security and be done with it, but this will cause problems with some Web sites. I am willing to give up a little privacy—not too much—for the sake of a more satisfying browsing experience.

To customize your own security preferences, load Internet Explorer. Then select **Tools | Internet Options**. Then click on the **Security** tab. Now click on the **Custom Level** button. Here are my settings:

ActiveX controls and plug-ins:
- Download signed ActiveX controls   Enable
- Download unsigned ActiveX controls   Disable
- Initialize and script ActiveX controls not marked as safe   Disable
- Run ActiveX controls and plug-ins   Prompt
- Script ActiveX controls marked safe for scripting   Prompt

Cookies:
- Allow cookies that are stored on your computer   Disable
- Allow per session cookies   Prompt

Downloads:
- File download   Disable
- Font download   Disable

Microsoft VM:
- Java permissions   High safety

Miscellaneous:
- Access data sources across domains   Disable

- Don't prompt for client certificate selection
  when no certificates or only one certificate exists   Disable
- Drag and drop or copy and paste files   Prompt
- Installation of desktop items   Disable
- Launching programs and files in an IFRAME   Disable
- Navigate sub-frames across different domains   Disable
- Software channel permissions   Disable
- Submit nonencrypted form data   Disable
- User data persistence   Disable

Scripting:
- Active scripting   Disable
- Allow paste operations via script   Disable
- Scripting of Java applets   Disable

User Authentication:
- Logon   Prompt for user name and password

SECOND AND THIRD DIMENSION STRATEGIES

So far we've discussed some First Dimension privacy issues. Let's move now to Second and Third Dimension privacy issues: protection from criminals, lawyers, hackers, and rogue government agencies. I won't differentiate between the Second and Third because they end up being one and the same when it comes to your computer and Internet usage.

Based on my analysis, there are ten specific threats you need to consider and protect yourself against. These are not listed in any particular order. If you want to protect your privacy, you will address each of them.

Threat #1: Someone steals your computer. Perhaps you think it is mainly the Internet that threatens computer privacy. Think again.

Computer theft is a significant problem in the United States. Almost a thousand laptops are stolen *every day*. Perhaps you did not realize how likely it is that your computer might be stolen, or just what is at stake. Yes, you could lose your computer and whatever projects you have been working on. But more importantly, a criminal could gain extensive knowledge about you and your family.

Once someone has your computer, he has access to a lot of information about you. Any application you have stored as a word-processing file could probably be used to steal your identity. And what about Quicken or Microsoft Money? If a thief gets into one of those two programs, the game is over. He most likely has everything he needs to bleed you dry. In addition, based on the information on your hard drive, a professional criminal could decide if it is worth breaking into your house. And a stalker would have a great head start if he could swipe your computer.

Even if you employ some level of password access, criminals can take as long as necessary to crack the codes. In fact, there are hundreds of Web sites devoted to cracking the passwords of all the most common applications, including Quicken and Microsoft Money. One such site is CRAK Software.[3] Its motto is "You hack 'em ... we crack 'em." The site claims to recover passwords for Word, Excel, QuickBooks, Quicken, Money, and scores of other programs.

(Incidentally, for the time being I am not considering the fact that someone with access to your computer can read even the files you have deleted. We will deal with this threat below.)

The most obvious response to the threat of computer theft is to take steps to prevent unauthorized access to your home or place of business. This may be common sense, but, quite frankly, common sense is in short supply. My hope is that identity theft and other invasions of privacy will motivate you to protect yourself. You can lose more than a machine; you can lose your privacy. Make sure you keep your doors locked, and, if you have a security system, use it. (You do have a security system, don't you?)

Don't forget that your work computer can also be stolen. If it has any personal information in it, then the theft of that computer could cost you more than it does your employer. If you are able to lock your office at night, make sure you do so. You might also make a point of *not* keeping more info than necessary on such a vulnerable computer.

For laptops—the computers that are most likely to be stolen— you can secure your computer to a desk using a cable lock. You may not realize this, but most laptops contain a security device that allows them to be attached to something that is fixed in place. The cable lock fits in that mechanism and can then be attached to a desk or any other convenient heavy object. I recommend the DefCon Cable Lock,[4] which is a galvanized steel cable that cannot be easily cut. The device features a four-digit combination lock with ten thousand possible combinations so that the owner doesn't have to worry about losing a key. The lock is very easy to use because it fits into the security lock slot of most computers, and, at only 6.2 ounces, it is lightweight and perfect for travel. This particular cable lock currently sells for $29.99 and can be purchased at most computer retailers, such as CompUSA, or directly from Targus, the manufacturer.

Obviously, you should never leave your laptop unattended in a public place. But what if you're using your computer in the Delta Crown Room or the public library and you simply *have* to use the bathroom? If you must leave your computer unattended, use an alarm system, which substantially reduces the risk of theft. Again, Targus makes the product I use, the DefCon 1 Notebook Security

Alarm,[5] which costs just $49.99. This alarm, which uses a conventional nine-volt battery, easily attaches to your carrying case, luggage, or any computer with a security lock slot, and it is very simple to use but difficult for thieves to disarm. A motion detector (which can be set at low or high sensitivity) triggers a high-pitched 110 decibel alarm, as will any severed cable. The device also uses a combination lock with a thousand different combinations, and since it is about the size of a cell phone it is ideal for travel.

Threat #2: Someone copies information directly off your computer. If you do what I have suggested above, you will keep someone from walking off with your computer. But thieves can also steal your data without ever moving your computer.

If you leave your computer unattended while in a hotel room, a library, or anywhere else, someone can simply sit down and start viewing—or even copying—your files. This can also happen at the workplace. Perhaps your computer is accessible while you are in a meeting or at lunch, or perhaps to one of the janitors at night.

Okay, so maybe you protect your computer with a password. But it really depends on how you implement it. Most computers have three built-in password options:

1. *The boot-up password.* This is usually set in your computer's CMOS, the chip that retains your system settings even when the power is off. CMOS RAM stores information your computer needs when it boots up, such as hard drive types, keyboard and display type, chip set, and even the time and date. Obviously, however, this password won't work when you allow your computer to remain on but unattended. Worse, it is rather simple to bypass this limited security device. Simply removing the CMOS battery can defeat the

password. When you do this, all the information stored in CMOS is lost and the system defaults to the factory settings—with no password. Nevertheless, I suggest you use the boot-up password because there are many potential violators who don't have the knowledge or patience to get past this security device. Be sure to turn your computer off before you leave work for the day.

2. *The Windows password.* This safeguard feature is pretty worthless. Simply hitting the escape key and canceling out of the password dialog box easily defeats it. The passwords for Windows 2000 and NT are a little better and can't be defeated so easily. Regardless, you should still use this password because it will deter anyone who doesn't have the knowledge to bypass it.

3. *A screensaver password.* This will protect you when you step away from your desk while your computer is still running. Of course, simply rebooting the computer can defeat this password, but it will discourage the unsophisticated and the merely curious—and that's about all.

I recommend that you acquire a system that does a better job than any of the three password features that come with your computer. A custom password solution like DesktopShield2000 can't be defeated by rebooting or tampering with the CMOS. Not only can you not afford to do without this, but you can easily afford it—it's free on software developer Stéphane Groleau's Web site (www.crosswinds.net/~steff3). With this safety device, the computer cannot be rebooted, and the password can't be bypassed. Moreover, DesktopShield2000 automatically locks the desktop after Windows starts, and it starts the screensaver after a user-designated time. Even the settings are protected by a password; in other words, a user can't change the password without the password. The device also logs all unsuccessful access attempts in a file, and it allows one-click starting—that is, the user can simply click on the icon in the system tray to start the screensaver.

Threat #3: Someone sends you an e-mail attachment that is infected with a virus. Having dealt with the threats that are present to your computer and to your privacy physically, we need to consider cyberspace threats. The most prominent of these is a virus that infects your computer and destroys your data.

In May of 2000, Reuters reported that the "love" bug—a virus spread by e-mails saying "ILOVEYOU" in the subject line—had cost $5 billion and that it would cost another $5 billion before all the damage was fixed.[6] This virus was so devastating because not only did it damage the recipient's computer but it then sent itself by e-mail to everyone in that person's address book. Even worse, once everyone had learned of the ILOVEYOU virus and developed ways of dealing with it, a mutation appeared that had different words in the subject line and that the antivirus software developed for the original bug couldn't stop.[7] Within a day there were at least seven more viruses.[8]

How did these mutations develop? People maliciously altered the code in the original virus and sent it back out onto the Internet to do more damage. As the senior product manager for F-Secure, Steve Gottwals, commented, "There's a big hacker community out there, and anyone could open up the script. It's really easy to make a variant."[9] If it is easy to do, someone on the Web will do it.

But viruses don't just damage or destroy computers; they can invade your privacy as well. One problem is Trojan Horses, such as BackDoor-G2.svr.21,[10] which enter your system and transmit information—including passwords—back to the creator. They get into your computer by posing as a safe program that is e-mailed to you or, more likely, that you think you want to download from a Web site. Even more dangerous software programs such as BackOrifice,[11] put out by the hacker group "Cult of the Dead Cow,"[12] enable another user anywhere on the Web to control your computer.

The first rule to remember is this: *do not open e-mail attachments from people you don't know*. That is the easiest way to get a virus. Besides, don't you have better things to do with your time than read unsolicited e-mail from strangers?

The second rule is: *do not open unsolicited e-mail attachments even from people you know unless you are expecting those attachments*. The major reason the ILOVEYOU was so effective was that people received infected e-mails from their friends, family, and acquaintances. As a result, people let down their guard and opened the messages.

Incidentally, one easy way to spread a virus is to send an e-mail that provides some pretext to get the recipient to forward it to all his friends. E-mail involving cute stories, urban-myth warnings about all sorts of dangers, or even warnings about a dangerous virus can all be a strategy to spread a virus. As a rule, it is good policy *not* to forward such material. (And aren't you getting tired of receiving forwarded e-mails yourself?)

The third and final rule is: *install a good virus protection program*. There is more than one available on the Internet. I recommend Norton AntiVirus. At this writing, it retails for $39.95, but I've seen it at discount clubs for about $20. Norton AntiVirus automatically scans incoming attachments—before they even enter your e-mail software; it looks for and removes Trojan Horse programs; it works on compressed files; and it is easy to keep updated, since updates can be scheduled as an automatic process.

Whatever program you end up using, make sure you update it on a weekly basis. (Most programs allow you to schedule automatic updates.) This is necessary because hackers are constantly creating new viruses.

Threat #4: Someone intercepts a compromising e-mail message you have sent and obtains sensitive information. Several problems can result from what you send out on the Internet.

E-mail messages are passed between "routers"—that is, from one computer to another on the Internet—as they make their way to their final destination. A message can be intercepted and read at any point along the way. In this sense, sending an e-mail is much more like mailing a traditional postcard than a letter. A program like the FBI's Carnivore can intercept messages, as can hackers who use so-called "packet-sniffing" tools.[13] Anyone can trace your e-mail messages back to you, using the e-mail headers. Someone with the right tools can even retrieve your name and password.[14]

How do you protect yourself? Just as abstinence is the best "safe sex" method, the only way to *guarantee* that your private information won't be intercepted on the Internet is not to send sensitive information on the Web. This doesn't mean you can't communicate at all; it merely means that you must think twice before sending a sensitive message via e-mail—especially something like an account number. You need to get "old-fashioned." Say you want to make a purchase with a credit card. If the site does not offer a secure server feature, you can always phone in your order (following the precautions given in Chapter 12) or use traditional mail. You could even avoid the credit card payment completely and achieve ultraprivacy through face-to-face communication. If you see a book on the Internet that you want, you can usually get a local retail outlet to order it for you at about the same price.

E-mail is convenient, however, and there are ways you can continue to use it while reducing the risk of having your privacy compromised. In fact, with current encryption technologies, e-mail is actually one of the *most* secure methods of communication available. Pretty Good Privacy (PGP) is an excellent program, but I've found that people have difficulty setting it up and using it. Fortunately, a couple of new products have made sending encrypted e-mail easier. My favorite is HushMail.com, which enables users to exchange encrypted e-mail using a Web-based interface. You don't have to know anything about public keys, encryption, or anything else. The program handles all the details, allowing you to communicate privately and securely with other HushMail users.[15] HushMail uses 1024-bit encryption, the strongest available, and it can also notify you when you have received an encrypted message. Best of all, it's free. To use HushMail, simply get your friends to sign up. Whenever you have something private or sensitive to communicate, use your HushMail account.

Threat #5: Someone gains access to your system by guessing or cracking your password. Amazingly, more than 50 percent of all computer users use the word "password" as their primary password. Worse, system administrators, who should know better, often use the word "admin" as their password. If you fall into either of these categories, shame on you!

Fortunately, it is not difficult to create an almost uncrackable password. Start by observing the following rules:

Rule #1: Don't use common words. This includes words like "password," "admin," your first name, your last name, your mother's maiden name, or your birth date. These are the first passwords that would-be hackers will try.

Rule #2: Don't use real words. Instead use a combination of letters, numbers, and punctuation. Do not use a simple word that can be found in the dictionary. Many password-cracking programs simply feed words from a dictionary to the appropriate target field until they get a match. Making up a password will neutralize most of these programs.

Rule #3: Don't use a password at all—instead use a pass phrase. Instead of "joH35&#4" (which is actually pretty good), try something like "the rabbit went down the hole&#$@" (which is better). Better yet, make up a nonsensical phrase: "rabbits and fry! gauge military whomp#@^!" In general, the longer the password, the more difficult it is to crack. Pass phrases are even more difficult. Unfortunately, many programs restrict the length of the password. When this happens, do the best you can with Rule #2.

Rule #4: Don't use the same password for every application. If you do, once someone cracks one password, he has effectively cracked all of them. You have handed over the keys to your kingdom. Instead create a different password for each application.

Perhaps you're thinking, *But how can I keep track of all these passwords?* Good question. Fortunately, programmers have written software for just this purpose. You have a couple of options.

First, you can download and use a program like Password Officer.[16] This program has a number of excellent features. First, it will automatically create a password for you (following Rule #2) or allow you to enter one manually. In addition, it uses "twofish" 256-bit key strong encryption—one of the very best available—to protect your password file. It can also be used with a smart card so that no one can access the program without knowing both the password and physically inserting the smart card. The program can be run at start-up, requiring the user to enter the master password to access it. The only problem with this solution, especially if you use it without a smart card, is that *if* someone cracks your master password and gains access to your password file, you're in big trouble. That person then has access to *all* your passwords.

A better option is Pins.Steganos.com,[17] a free, Web-based solution that provides a number of advantages over a program stored on your hard drive. With this, registration is totally anonymous. Even though you are storing all your passwords on someone else's server, there is no way anyone can link these back to you. All the service has is your master user ID and password, which can be anything you want. You can access your passwords from anywhere in the world, as long as you can get to a computer with Internet access. You can even use a WAP-compatible mobile phone. And the server is, of course, encrypted. The only two disadvantages, compared to Password Officer, are that it won't automatically create passwords for you and it won't feed the passwords to the appropriate applications.

Threat #6: Someone gains entry into your system via the Internet. Believe it or not, hackers can gain access to your computer through your Internet connection. Scores of programs automatically search the Internet for users with unsecured connections. When they find one, hackers can take control of the computer, download files, upload files, and more.

To find out how vulnerable your computer is, visit Gibson Research's "Shields UP!" Web site (grc.com/x/ne.dll?bh0bkyd2). This site will evaluate your Internet connection security. Unless you are running a personal firewall program, the results will shock you. You are probably far more vulnerable than you realize. Connecting to the Internet without a firewall is the Web equivalent of living in a high-crime district without locks on your doors and windows. It's only a matter of time before someone breaks in and wreaks havoc.

You can obtain complete protection—something Shields UP! refers to as "full stealth mode"—by downloading and installing ZoneAlarm, a personal firewall program. This program provides a dynamic firewall to control the door to your computer and to maintain your PC's invisibility to the Internet and potential intruders; application control to ensure that rogue applications cannot send your valuable data to criminals and vandals; Security Levels that automatically configure the firewall and handle all the details; Local and Internet Zones that give you the convenience of sharing important data with trusted people while denying the privilege to everyone else; and MailSafe-Email Attachment Protection to thwart e-mail Visual Basic Script (VBS) worms, such as the ILOVEYOU virus. Finally, ZoneAlarm provides Internet Lock to block Internet traffic while your PC is unattended or not utilizing the Internet; many Internet connections, such as cable modem or DSL, are always on, and this gives you total control over your connection.[18] Combined, these elements guarantee secure Internet use because each one is stronger than if it were used alone. The other advantage of this program is that it's free. I've been using it for several months, and it works flawlessly. This is one of the most important programs you can add to your system, especially if you are using an "always-on" Internet connection.

Threat #7: Someone monitors your recent activity while on the computer. Your computer has a near-perfect memory. It monitors—and logs—virtually everything you do. For example, did you know: Every click on your Windows 98 start menu is logged and permanently stored on a hidden encrypted database within your computer? Every Web page, picture, sound, and e-mail you have ever downloaded or transmitted can easily be recovered by forensic analysis programs like EnCase[19] or F.R.E.D.?[20] Every file you have ever loaded in a specific application is recorded?

Using these Windows "features," anyone can create a profile of your activity and learn an amazing amount about your habits, preferences, and contacts.

The best program I have found for dealing with "digital tracks" is Evidence Eliminator. At this writing it sells for $74.95, but it is worth every penny.[21] It does what no other program I am aware of does. Specifically, it destroys the following in one click:

- Windows SWAP file
- Windows Application logs
- Windows Temporary files
- Windows Recycle Bin
- Windows Registry backups
- Windows Clipboard data
- Start Menu Recent Documents history
- Start Menu Run history
- Start Menu Find Files history
- Start Menu Find Computer history
- Start Menu Order data
- Start Menu Click history
- Microsoft Internet Explorer temporary typed URLs, index files, cache, and history
- Microsoft Internet Explorer AutoComplete memory of form posts and passwords
- Microsoft Internet Explorer cookies (selective cookie keeping for versions 5 and above)

- Microsoft Internet Explorer Internet components (selective keeping of components)
- Microsoft Internet Explorer Download Folder memory
- Microsoft Internet Explorer Favorites List
- Microsoft Outlook Express v5+ database (selective keeping of mail and newsgroups)
- Windows Media Player history
- Windows Media Player PlayLists in Media Library
- America OnLine Instant Messenger contacts
- Netscape Navigator temporary typed URLs, files, cache, and history
- Netscape Navigator cookies (selective cookie keeping for versions 4 and above)
- Netscape Mail v4+ sent and deleted e-mails
- Netscape Mail hidden files
- Customizable lists of files and folders, with or without their contents
- Customizable scan lists of file types in specific folders
- Customizable scan lists of file types on all drives
- Deleted file names, sizes, and attributes from drive directory structures
- Free cluster space ("Slack") from all file tips
- Magnetic remnants from underneath existing files/folders
- All free unallocated space on all hard drives
- Evidence of activity in many other programs, using Plug-In modules
- Slack space and deleted entries in the Windows registry
- Created and modified dates and times on all files and folders
- Windows Registry Streams
- Common Dialog load/save location history

Threat #8: Someone peeks into your most sensitive data files. Even when you're using a series of passwords that will keep all but the truly committed out of your computer, it is wise to have certain files and/or directories encrypted.

I suggest that you create a special file folder for highly sensitive files. This is where you will store things like your financial files, correspondence, and other personal files. You will then need to download a program that will encrypt and decrypt your files at your discretion. You can find hundreds of these encryption programs on the Internet. Some of them are free; some are quite expensive. There's not necessarily a relationship between price and quality.

The program I use is CryptoMite, a shareware program that sells for just $29.[22] You can try it free for thirty days. This provides high-performance, unbroken encryption algorithms (Blowfish, DES), seamless integration with the Windows desktop, and user-friendly interface. In addition, it encrypts complete folders with all subfolders; creates self-extracting, encrypted, and compressed EXE (executable) files; hides complete disk drives; and locks single EXE-files with a password (no encryption necessary).

Threat #9: Someone reconstructs your deleted data files. Most people don't realize that they must worry about sensitive data they have deleted from their computer. The fact is that everything you have ever put on your computer—even if you have thrown it away—can be recovered with the appropriate technology. If someone steals your computer and wants to find what you have been doing on- or offline, he can find anything, including files deleted many years earlier.

To protect yourself, you can choose from a number of programs that obliterate the remains of deleted files, including Evidence Eliminator, which I recommended under Threat #7 above. Other stand-alone programs do just as well. One such program is Shredder95/98/NT, which can shred your deleted files beyond recovery.[23] It conforms to the Department of Defense (DOD) standard for file deletion, shreds multiple files as well as entire folders and directories, deletes free space, and has an easy-to-use interface. This program is sold in three editions—Basic, Standard, and Professional—priced from $29.95 to $49.95. Though it's the most expensive, I recommend the Professional edition because it has double the level of shredding security, goes beyond the DOD standards, removes all trace of the original file (date, time, size, and name), and makes recovery of physical or magnetic data impossible.

Threat #10: Someone at your ISP uses Caller ID to identify your phone number and does a reverse search to locate you. While the possibility of this happening is somewhat remote, it's quite easy to do.

Try this little exercise. Go to AnyWho.com. Click on "Reverse Lookup." Now enter your phone number. Chances are the next thing you will see is your name and address. (If you don't see this, congratulations. You are doing something right!) The fun is only beginning. If you click on the "Maps" link, the program will provide you with a detailed map and specific directions on how to get to your house. This is a stalker's dream come true. (In Chapter 9, I will show you how to keep anything from showing up on these kinds of searches.) It's amazing to me that sites like AnyWho.com haven't been sued. I'm confident it's only a matter of time.

Fortunately, protecting yourself from this kind of problem is fairly simple—at least as it pertains to people who don't already have your phone number. First, check with your phone company to see what options are available. If possible, order a service called "per line blocking," which prevents Caller IDs from revealing your phone number. If this service is not available in your area, then you can usually block your ID on a per call basis. For example, to keep my number from being revealed, I must enter "*67" before dialing the phone number. (This may be different in your particular area, so check with your service provider.) You can enter this code directly into your dial-up connection so that it is invoked every time you connect to the Internet. (Make sure to add a comma after the "*67"; this tells the modem to pause before dialing the phone number.)

CONCLUSION

Obviously, no one can make himself beyond risk. No one is invisible or invulnerable. But if you address these issues by taking the proper steps and following the right procedures, your privacy will become much harder to penetrate, and you will be a far less inviting target.

You should recognize that for as little as $250 you can achieve the highest level of privacy protection.

PRACTICAL PRIVACY TIP #11:
Secure Third Dimension Computer Privacy for Less Than $250

By purchasing and installing the following products, you will be able to operate your computer with near-total privacy.

Product	Available From	Price
GuideScope	http://www.junkbusters.com/ht/en/guidescope.html	FREE
DefCon CL Cable Lock	Most computer retailers or directly from Targus	$29.99
DefCon 1 Notebook Security Alarm	Most computer retailers or directly from Targus	$49.99
DesktopShield2000	http://www.crosswinds.net/~steff3	FREE
Norton AntiVirus	Most computer retailers	$39.95
HushMail.com	http://www.hushmail.com	FREE
Pins.Steganos.Com	http://steganos.com	FREE
ZoneAlarm	http://www.zonealarm.com	FREE
Evidence Eliminator	http://www.evidence-eliminator.com	$74.95
CryptoMite— Professional Edition*	http://www.baxbex.com/cryptomite.htm	$49.95
	Total Cost	$244.83

* Optional

CHAPTER EIGHT
BANKING AND FINANCES

The banks ... have the regulation of the safety-valves of our fortunes, and ... condense and explode them at their will.
—Thomas Jefferson

Financial privacy in the United States is virtually nonexistent. The exceptions prove the rule. Alaska and Vermont are known for having strict laws regarding what information banks and other financial institutions can tell about you.[1] Those two states stand out from all the others in this respect.

Vermont has had a law since 1995 prohibiting banks from giving out private information without permission in writing from the customer. Even with twenty-four exceptions to the rule, it is still much better than what virtually every other state has. In general, Vermont seems to be very conscious of privacy issues since banks were remarkably tight-lipped even before the law was passed. According to one bank official, banks will not even reveal if a customer has an account there.[2]

The Alaska Banking Code has forbidden banks from sharing information since before the 1970s. Alaska's law is even more comprehensive than Vermont's. Court orders and subpoenas are the only two exceptions to a blanket prohibition on revealing customer information without prior written consent.[3] In all, the banks seem quite willing to protect their customers' privacy, believing that privacy benefits rather than hurts them.

Both the media and the government continue to promote a privacy stereotype: *anyone who objects to the efforts of state surveillance must have something to hide*. But the laws and attitudes in Alaska and Vermont demonstrate that people who are not engaged in criminal activity such as money laundering or tax evasion can value privacy. Do Alaska and Vermont put a premium on privacy because their residents are criminals wanting to evade detection? Doubtful. Most residents of those two states are people like you and me who simply mind their own business and believe that others should do the same.

Just because we oppose the network of reporting mandates and computer-monitoring programs doesn't mean we should be regarded with suspicion. We have the right *not* to be scrutinized in our affairs, *not* to be treated as criminals who must be watched.

But the sad reality is that we are being watched. Organizations are encouraged, and in some cases rewarded, for reporting "suspicious behavior." So we must protect ourselves.

THE NEED FOR FINANCIAL PRIVACY

More than 98 percent of all financial transactions are digital. As a result, all of your checks, credit card transactions, and wire transfers are recorded. A comprehensive list of your assets, liabilities, spending, and credit history is available to anyone with Internet access and as little as $29 to invest in a background check.

Remember, if an attorney is looking for a way to get a client damages from some incident, he will look at *everyone* who could possibly be involved in the incident, no matter how remotely, and target those with the deepest pockets. Privacy means financial protection not just from criminals but from predatory attorneys and their frivolous lawsuits as well.

Worse, the Treasury Department's FinCEN system (Financial Crimes Enforcement Network) gives the federal government the ability to track every nickel you spend—in real time. Anything that is supposedly out of the ordinary raises a flag in the system, enabling the government to take immediate action, including freezing your accounts or seizing your assets. Again, even if you haven't done anything wrong, you could suffer simply for doing something that *appears* suspicious. Even if you are later cleared, you could suffer financial ruin.

FIRST DIMENSION STRATEGIES

If you want to pursue First Dimension privacy (as defined in Chapter 5), there are a couple of things you can do to protect yourself.

Use Cash as Much as Possible

Making your purchases through ordering seems convenient. Products are brought directly to your door. You can access a wider selection than might be available at your local store.

Or so it seems.

Retail establishments carry many of the items you're probably ordering. And if they don't, they can order items just as easily as you can. The principle here is simple: *use retailers as a shield to protect your identity*. Why should your purchasing profile be available to anyone who wants it? If you use cash, there is no need for anyone to have access to your identity.[4] If a store insists on having your name and phone number when you order something, you can always provide an alias and your secondary phone number.

Avoid Membership in Retailers' Card Schemes

Imagine that one day you are in court and a lawyer wants to undermine your credibility and assault your character in front of the jury. How would you feel if, while you were on the stand, the lawyer began asking you about every purchase you had made at your local grocery store, even though you had used cash to make the purchases?

Seem implausible?

A friend of mine found himself in just this predicament in the middle of a divorce case. His wife's lawyer managed to get a record of all his purchases. How? My friend had used the supermarket's discount card, which tracked his every purchase. The fact that he routinely bought expensive red wine was used against him because he had argued that he could barely make ends meet and thus couldn't afford more alimony.

Discount cards are indeed a threat to your privacy. In signing you up, stores often ask rather intrusive questions about where you live and sometimes even insist on getting your Social Security number. That alone should make you think twice about joining. But the biggest concern is that when you use a discount card you are leaving an electronic record of each and every item you buy— and an adversary can use your past transactions against you. Using cash does nothing to conceal your anonymity if you swipe your membership card every time you make a purchase. As the privacy group CASPIAN (Consumers Against Supermarket Privacy Invasion and Numbering) observes, these card membership systems are basically "registration and monitoring programs."[5]

PRACTICAL PRIVACY TIP #12:
Don't Use a Fake Discount Shopping Card

Some people think they can evade supermarkets' surveillance schemes and still receive the benefits of a discount card by signing up under a false name. Katherine Albrecht, the founder of CASPIAN (Consumers Against Supermarket Privacy Invasion and Numbering), offers key reasons why this is not a good idea:[6]

1. **It is a selfish solution.** By signing up under a fake name you acknowledge that there is a problem but leave it for the next person to solve. Avoid these cards altogether—and better yet, boycott stores that implement such systems.

2. **It makes the problem worse.** If you hand over a card every time you're asked to, whether it's fake or not, you simply go on the store's books as one more happy shopper. And supermarkets often point to their many "satisfied customers" as proof that people love these programs.

3. **It feeds the hand that bites you.** By patronizing an offending store, you're financially supporting a company whose policies you oppose.

4. **It contributes to the pervasive image that such programs are okay.** Other shoppers will obviously see you using a discount card.

5. **It makes you complacent.** Because you think you've found "the solution," you no longer feel as if you have to fight, and you'll simply avoid the underlying issues.

6. **It is a weak approach.** By avoiding discount cards—and perhaps avoiding the stores themselves—you will be taking a stand, living by the principles you profess.

7. **You may not be able to get a false card.** Many supermarkets require you to show a state-issued photo ID card or provide a

> Social Security number (or probably both), so falsifying information on an application simply may not work.
> 8. **It could eventually force stores to ask for *more* information.** If a store discovers many fake records in its database, it may implement even more invasive scrutiny techniques.

In short, if you are dealing in cash and want to protect your privacy, don't join these discount card membership clubs. Besides, they promise great discounts but actually deliver very little. Are they worth your privacy?

One other note: don't be tempted to sign up for such programs using an alias. This only encourages the privacy-violating tactics. For the sake of all of us, it's better to protest the practice and refuse to participate. If you're really committed to protesting these schemes, you may want to boycott stores that have discount card systems. (See CASPIAN's Web site, at www.nocards.org, for a rating of all grocery chains in terms of privacy.)

Money Orders

One way to carry out long-distance financial transactions is to go to the post office and pay in cash for a money order. Money orders are totally anonymous because you are not required to show any ID, and you'll leave no record of the transaction. If you order an item using a money order and have this item sent to a mail drop under an assumed name, there will be no trace of the transaction easily available to anyone. You are not put in a database. You are not profiled according to your purchasing habits.

More than 20 percent of American households do not have a checking account.[7] These people must use money orders for routine payments, so the practice is well established. The only downside that I am aware of is that you are limited to $700 per money order. You can purchase multiple money orders, but up to only $10,000 per day. In addition, you should note that if you purchase more than $3,000, federal law requires you to fill out Form 8105-A, Funds Transactional Transfer Report.

Use Different Financial Institutions

When it comes to financial services, do *not* pursue "one-stop shopping." Due to some recent changes in the laws and the many mergers among banks, brokerage houses, and so on, multiple financial services are now often offered under one roof.[8] Charles Schwab, for example, offers "banking, checking, bill payment, brokerage, mutual funds, loans, insurance and annuities."[9] Schwab and other such companies market the *convenience* of this kind of comprehensive service.

Yes, it is convenient, but it is also extremely risky to your privacy. If you use one company, it will know everything about your finances—how you spend your money, how much debt you are shouldering, how you make your decisions. True, the company will then be in a position to offer you financial goods and services that you might want, but it will also be in a position to manipulate you, to convince you to buy more and more. The further risk is that the company will sell its information about you. Beyond all that, if you are completely financially dependent on one company, you will find it very hard to take your business elsewhere. If you are going to different companies for financial services, then you can move, say, your mutual funds from one company to another with relative ease.

SECOND DIMENSION STRATEGIES

The key to evading the systems of surveillance that exist in our society is to use a separate entity for all transactions. In other

words: *never do business in your own name*. You must assume the pos-
ture of an agent of some other entity, acting not on your own
behalf but on behalf of the entity you represent—be it a Limited
Liability Company (LLC), a trust, an International Business
Corporation (IBC), or something else.

All these options have benefits as well as dangers. Let's look at
them one at a time.

Limited Liability Companies

A Limited Liability Company (LLC) is a legal entity that is
separate from the LLC's owners (often called "members"). It is a
cross between a corporation and a partnership because the members of an LLC are protected from personal liability, though prof-
its and losses are passed directly to members and the LLC itself
isn't taxed. An LLC's primary purpose is to allow you to start a
business but protect your personal assets if that business gets sued.
The property of the LLC could be confiscated or forfeited, but
your personal property is safe.

Thus, LLCs are normally thought of as a means of asset protection. In fact, in some states only one person is required to form
an LLC. You can reduce your taxes and liability by forming an
LLC, transferring your business assets to that corporation, and
then having the corporation lease the assets back to your original
company. Furthermore, depending on the laws in your own state,
you can also form an LLC in another state and get the protections
afforded by that state's laws. This could mean lower taxation levels
and a choice of which state laws will apply to the actions of the
LLC. Nevada, Wyoming, and Delaware in particular have laws
favorable to LLCs.

Perhaps the most important advantage is that an LLC lets you
protect your privacy because you can often form and run one

anonymously. In many cases you can appoint other officers so that your name doesn't appear on any of the LLC's public records. For the ultimate in privacy, you should order this so-called nominee service through your attorney. All correspondence and communication should come through your attorney. Although this is more expensive (you are now paying two lawyers—the first attorney hires the second to form the LLC), it preserves the confidentiality inherent in the attorney-client privilege.

Because there is a real market for these entities, you have plenty of options for researching and ultimately starting an LLC. On the Internet you will find local companies as well as ones in Nevada, Wyoming, and Delaware. One such online company is Corporate Service Center at www.corporateservicecenter.com. This site will give you a good education on LLCs and even assist you in setting one up. (You can actually have an LLC created online for as little as $300.) It also discusses the various jurisdictions and the advantages and disadvantages of incorporating in each.

One caveat, however: Because LLCs are relatively new, there is some concern about how courts will treat them when cases arise. There is not much legal precedent. Furthermore, just because you are protected by an LLC does not mean you can do anything immoral or illegal behind your corporate mask. The corporate protection can be removed.[10]

Nevertheless, LLCs are a good way to protect your privacy, since they allow you to transact business without leaving a record of your identity.

Trusts

Trusts are another option for reclaiming your privacy. They are basically agreements to benefit certain people. Anywhere the law allows people to engage in contracts, trusts are recognized.

Indeed, trusts have a life of their own—often outlasting those who formed them, since trusts are commonly used to provide for descendants.

Though there are many different kinds of trusts, the two basic types are statutory trusts and common-law or pure trusts. Statutory trusts operate based on state laws and regulations, whereas pure trusts are simply based on our common-law heritage, on people's right to make contracts.[11]

Privacy author Larry Sontag writes:

> Exchanging property into a pure trust is *not* a taxable event. They do not operate under any government laws or regulations and have no accounting, withholding, or Social Security requirements. They do not require or have Social Security numbers, EIN's, TIN's, or any other federal ID numbers and can operate in complete confidentiality. Financial institutions may, however, require identification numbers if the Trust resides in the United States and attempts to open up a bank or brokerage account, or if it purchases or sells real estate. Information about the assets, liabilities, and management of these trusts is completely confidential and not accessible to the government or to the public. The corpus (assets of these trusts) cannot be threatened, seized, liened, or levied because of any debt or obligation incurred by the Trustees or the Beneficiaries. Trustees and Beneficiaries are not liable for the debts of these trusts.[12]

Despite all the legal protections or immunities that a trust has, a trust formed in this country can still be investigated and its privacy violated, just as a person's can be. So you might consider forming a foreign grantor trust—that is, a trust in another country. Many options are available, but a full discussion of trusts is beyond the

scope of this book. If you are interested, check out the current recommendations on my Web site at www.moreprivacy.com.

THIRD DIMENSION STRATEGIES

If you want the ultimate in privacy and asset protection, you
will probably need to go offshore. Entire books have been written
on this subject, so I won't go into great detail here. This is
intended to be an overview to get you started on the subject and
make you aware of the possibilities. Again, I have current recommendations on my Web site.

International Business Corporations

An International Business Corporation (IBC), like an LLC, is
a legal entity treated as a "person." It has a perpetual existence and
can sue or be sued. An IBC can do business anywhere outside its
country of origin (but not within) and is usually tax-exempt. It can
be used to buy or rent, own and operate businesses, maintain
checking accounts, hire employees, and do many other things.

In many countries IBCs do not need to reveal who the owners
or benefactors are. Investigating an IBC typically reveals the
name of the corporation, the date of incorporation, amendments,
and publicly filed documents, while shareholders and officers
remain anonymous.

IBCs are also very private because of their shares, either "bearer
shares" or "registered shares." Bearer shares are totally anonymous.
(If you have bearer shares, do not, under any circumstances, keep
them in or near any property that you own or that can be traced to
you.) Registered shares have the name of the owner on them, but
that name is on a registry available only to officers and shareholders.

IBCs depend on a registered agent, who is hired to represent
the company at a known physical address. That person receives

legal notices on behalf of the corporation and forwards them. Thus, once you form an IBC, you can use it to buy and sell without giving away your financial property.

Depending on your needs, you may want to consider complex structures that involve layers of IBCs, trusts, and LLCs. When set up by a professional, these can be very difficult if not impossible to pierce.

Offshore Banking

In his excellent book on offshore banking, Arnold Cornez writes:

> While the typical European child is multilingual and is raised in an environment where he or she may see a parent traipsing off to another country for business purposes just for the day, Americans by contrast are culturally and linguistically limited. Americans (including our U.S. Congress, with its "fortress America" hang-up) are seen from offshore as provincial and isolationists. Germans love to vacation, and some "live" to travel the world. At times I hear more German and German accents than English as I motor through Yosemite.
>
> Foreign nationals, other than the Reluctant American (RA), are also more inclined and comfortable in investing worldwide. The RA continues to self-restrict, at least in the geographic scope, by staying home. French and German business owners avoid what they perceive to be confiscatory income taxation by their respective countries by using offshore companies (conduits) to earn and retain a significant portion of the profits on each transaction (earnings stripping) through "upstreaming."...
> You need to psychologically adapt, to adjust and think globally, as the remainder of the world presently does. Let's catch up![13]

As Cornez illustrates, there really is nothing wrong with doing business in other countries—despite the common perception that "sunny climes are for shady people."[14] Think of it this way. If you live on the border of a state that taxes gasoline heavily, what's wrong with going down the road to fill up your tank in the other state at a significantly lower price?

In many ways the Internet is making borders irrelevant. Not only is it legal to invest your money in other countries, it is often greatly advantageous. Though people often associate offshore investing with illegal activity, I am not advocating anything illegal or even suspect. I believe you should pay every tax you owe, but you can protect your privacy by investing some of your money offshore.

Of course, offshore banking is not only a way to keep your finances private, it is also a way to support your other entities— LLCs, IBCs, and trusts. By having accounts overseas in the name of your IBC, you can be issued a corporate credit or debit card. Then you can keep your entire life private.

Be Careful Out There

Ultimately, what you are looking for in a bank is confidentiality, stability, and accessibility. The best way to achieve all of these is to use three or more banks because no one banking system in one location will have all three strengths.

Having recommended offshore banking and investing as ultimately the best way to protect your financial privacy, I want to caution you that it will take research, planning, and foresight. To find banks you know to be both safe and confidential requires a good deal of time and effort.

If you want to research this further, I highly recommend you go online and join the Offshore Privacy Club at www.permanenttourist.com. This will give practical, up-to-date

PRACTICAL PRIVACY TIP #13:
Understand Offshore Pros and Cons

Arnold Cornez, in his excellent *Offshore Money Book*, lists reasons to stay onshore and reasons to go offshore with your hard-earned money:

Why Bank and Invest in the U.S.?

1. There's nothing like the FDIC or FSLIC outside of the United States. The only way to insure an offshore bank is through a private insurer.
2. In the United States, the Securities Industry Protection Corporation, an agency of the federal government, insures you against losses from fraud.
3. Many investors outside the United States consider states like Nevada, Delaware, Wyoming, and Utah to be their safe havens.
4. The United States is the most stable country politically.
5. The maximum income tax rate at home is lower than that of many other industrialized countries.
6. Inflation is relatively low.
7. There are many estate planners in this country who can meet your needs for estate and financial planning.
8. There are no exchange controls for wiring money in the United States.
9. The U.S. dollar is still the currency used around the world. Cornez writes, "More hundred dollar bills circulate outside the U.S. than inside, by a ratio of about two to one."[15]

Why Bank and Invest Overseas?

1. Despite the advantages, we have less and less personal and financial privacy in the United States.

2. Diversity is a major principle of wise financial management; why not geopolitical diversity?

3. The United States is a litigation nightmare. If people can discover that you have deep pockets, you will likely become a target.

4. The United States may not always be as stable as it's been. What if some crisis hits the country or the economy goes bad?

5. Many questions remain about what will happen to the U.S. banking system as more and more banks are swallowed up in merger after merger.

6. In the United States there is a great deal of hidden taxation as well as unnecessary and costly regulation of businesses.

7. Domestic troubles might destroy your financial life. For instance, in a particularly acrimonious divorce your spouse might find a way to take everything you own.

8. You might need a reserve in case of business failure.

9. You might want to prepare in case of a serious illness.

10. You might want to provide for your retirement.

11. You might want to provide for your spouse and children after your death.

12. You might want to provide for a disabled spouse, or a child who is unable to support himself, or for some other person after your death.

13. You might want to protect a lump-sum disability award against potential claims by creditors.[16]

guidance on where you can safely put your money and how you can use it. It will cost you less than $120 per year, and the information and guidance you receive will be worth a great deal more than that. The site offers detailed advice from experienced professionals on how to conduct offshore banking, as well as continually updated news about what locations are safe, becoming safe, or no longer safe (that last category, sadly, is a growing one). Trust me: it's a whole lot cheaper than making mistakes on your own.

The Sovereign Society at www.sovereignsociety.com is another group that you can join for both information and connections. For less than $200 a year, it will connect you with safe offshore banks.

A Private Credit Card

Another way to ensure financial privacy is to use a foreign grantor trust to get an international credit card. A foreign-based card can be very private and leave no paper trail—if you do it right. Things may change, however. In the fall of 2000 a Miami court allowed the IRS to investigate the credit reports of thousands of Americans who held accounts in the Bahamas, the Cayman Islands, and the nation of Antigua and Barbuda.[17] Because the banks in question had headquarters in Miami, U.S. law could circumvent the foreign laws protecting customer privacy. (Incidentally, this means a person should avoid banks with branches in the United States.)

Still, you can protect yourself by getting an anonymous credit card or one in the name of another entity. Many companies provide this. Ideally, you want one issued in a country with better privacy laws than those of the three countries mentioned above. In addition, you want a card that is truly anonymous, not requiring your Social Security number or other identifying feature.

The landscape on this is constantly changing. Many organizations run scams that take advantage of the gullible and uninformed. Again, you can check www.moreprivacy.com for my latest recommendations.

CONCLUSION

Attaining financial privacy is difficult but not impossible. By using cash and money orders, avoiding discount shopping programs (which require you to register and then track your purchases), and using several financial vendors, you can secure a significant measure of privacy. This will get you perhaps 50 percent of the way toward total privacy.

Creating and using another entity—LLC or trust—will secure another 25 percent or so of your privacy.

But if you want near-total privacy, you will have to go offshore. Unfortunately, the number of places where you can safely store your money and still protect your privacy is shrinking. While American banks are often happy to shield the privacy of foreign account holders who come here for financial safe havens, their attitude suddenly changes when Americans begin taking their funds out of the country. It is important to remember this as you think about why you might go offshore, establish a trust, or incorporate an IBC.

The only way we are going to see lasting change in the trend toward reducing privacy is if more and more people refuse to accept the intrusions and insist on protecting their financial privacy.

The wealthy have been taking advantage of offshore banks, LLCs, IBCs, and trusts for years. With the rise of the Internet and the resultant cheap communication, most of us can now afford these structures. I know of no other way to attain such a high level of financial privacy.

CHAPTER NINE

YOUR PHYSICAL ADDRESS AND MAIL PRIVACY

*The real danger is the gradual erosion of individual liber-
ties through the automation, integration, and interconnec-
tion of many small, separate record-keeping systems, each of
which alone may seem innocuous, even benevolent, and
wholly justifiable.*

—U.S. Privacy Protection Study Commission, 1977

Even people that should know better can sometimes slip.
A close friend of mine, a minor celebrity, followed my
suggestions to the letter when having his main phone
line installed. He ordered the phone in the name of his trust and
gave his mail drop as the billing address. So far, so good.

A few months later, however, he ordered an ISDN line for his
house. He wanted to have fast Internet access, but broadband service (like cable or DSL) wasn't available in his rural location. So he
called the phone company and placed the order. Unfortunately, he

gave his real name to the person taking the order because he didn't even consider that the phone company would list an ISDN line. It did, but he had no idea and simply assumed that he was still invisible to the public.

Two months later a shaggy-haired man with several teeth missing pulled his rickety old pickup into my friend's driveway. The driver got out of the car and walked toward the front door. My friend's German shepherd instantly began growling, and his wife, answering the door, sensed that something was not quite right.

As it turned out, the man was a fan. He asked if this was the home of so-and-so. My friend's wife, already suspicious, denied it. The man, looking confused, then revealed how he had found the address. He had simply called information to get my friend's phone number. Then he used an Internet service to do a "reverse lookup." Bingo. My friend's address came up.

As you can imagine, as soon as the fan left, my friend called the phone company and had it delete his name from the account. He then waited an hour or so and called information just to make sure the problem had been corrected.

SAFE AT HOME

It can be dangerous to let people know where you live. Fortunately for my friend, nothing came of the problem. But what if the fan had been a stalker? As we've seen, there are plenty of reasons why someone might want to keep the location of his personal residence private: to avoid becoming a target of a frivolous lawsuit, to evade an abusive former spouse or other associate, or to be safe from the prying eye of unwanted media intrusion, to name a few.

To hide your physical address, you have to keep your mail private. That's why, in Chapter 6, I discussed a basic First Dimension strategy—namely, how you can use public drop boxes rather than

having mail sent directly to your house. Always use the street location of your drop-box service as your return address. By establishing a separate address for sending and receiving regular mail, you
can keep the location of your residence confidential. I can't
overemphasize the importance of this.

Securing a drop box is not the only way you can try to keep
the location of your residence private, however. Nor is it the only
way to prevent someone from going through your mail. In this
chapter I will move beyond First Dimension strategies and present
the full range of options for protecting your physical address as
well as your mail itself. Once again, it is up to you to decide how
much you want to do in pursuing privacy. Not all of these options
are for everyone. Indeed, many will not opt for the strategies I discuss here. While these strategies will take time and money to
implement, they do offer the utmost privacy available.

NON-OWNERSHIP

I know, all your life you've been taught the value of ownership.
If you don't own it, you can't control it; if you don't own it, you
can't enjoy the appreciation of the asset, and so forth. But we need
to rethink this advice in an age when our privacy is under attack.

Right now, if anyone wants to know about you and has some
basic piece of information—perhaps only a name and a phone
number where you can be reached and perhaps a rough idea of
where you live—he can get a detective agency to do a title search
and find out your exact location. Your property is always a matter
of public record.

But what if you don't own any?

What if you have exchanged your property into a trust—best
of all a trust formed in another nation? If that trust, in keeping
with its purpose of providing for the beneficiary, offers to let you

live in the house on the property, then you will simply live there as a tenant. If a stalker wants to find you, or an attorney wants to see how much he could get from you in a lawsuit, he won't be able to use public records to find out where you live. The only way he could find where you live is by following you.

In the last chapter I discussed how to create trusts, and, as you saw, the process can be fairly straightforward. One thing to keep in mind as you consider moving toward non-ownership is that you will not always get the best advice from lawyers on the subject. Why? It's generally not in a lawyer's interests for you to learn how trusts can protect you from probate—the source of so much of the legal profession's income. As Norman Dacey pointed out in his book *How to Avoid Probate* (which some New York lawyers unsuccessfully attempted to ban), "Probate is essentially a form of private taxation levied by the legal profession upon the rest of the population."[1] And besides, Dacey argued, few attorneys understand living trusts to begin with.[2]

So, despite what many in the legal profession would have you think, the use of trusts is an excellent way for you to protect your financial and other kinds of privacy. The very wealthy have been using trusts for years, but today using trusts to protect one's privacy is becoming a middle-class phenomenon.

Putting It in Trust

Essentially, to protect your privacy you put your property into a trust. You can do this through a simple quitclaim deed. The trust may then hire you as the managing director and allow you to live in the house as part of your compensation. Or it may simply rent the house to you. Electricity, water, cable TV, and other utilities can be listed in the name of the trust as well. To maintain your privacy, be sure that only items in the name of the trust are delivered to your residence; all others should go to your mail drop. (As a matter of policy, I don't have anything delivered to my home, period.) With trusts, you must be careful. If you put everything into one trust, you will be more vulnerable. For example, if all your assets are in one trust and that trust gets sued, you might lose everything. But if you transfer items into different trusts, your risk is reduced. Let's assume you have one trust to hold your real estate and another to hold your vehicles. If an automobile owned by the vehicle trust is in an accident and a lawyer decides to sue the trust, the only assets available will be those of that particular trust. More importantly, the court battle won't destroy your privacy. The trust owning the vehicle will be the only entity involved. Your other trusts won't even come into the picture.

Disciplines

Earlier in this book I talked about the disciplines necessary for protecting privacy. Transferring titles to your property into a trust makes some new disciplines essential.

How to Talk

If you transfer your car into a trust, then it is no longer your car. You must not call it your car. You must explain to your children that it is not your car. It does not belong to you. You are just permitted to use it. Your speaking habits need to match reality.

The same is true of everything else that you transfer into a trust. When you sign the quitclaim deed over to your trust, it is no longer your house. If you purchase an automobile with trust funds, it is not your car. You simply have use of the asset as managing director or some other officer of the trust. If you worked at home before you signed the quitclaim document, then you now live at your workplace. This will work quite nicely because the business will be owned by the trust, which will contract with other companies or persons for your labor. They will be contracting not with you personally but with the trust. Make sure you don't say otherwise.

If a salesman comes to your door and asks to see the owner of the house, you must tell him that you are simply the tenant.

How to Treat the Mail Appropriately

Anything that comes to the trust's house addressed to you personally needs to be marked "wrong address" and refused. All personal mail needs to go to your mail drop. Only the trust should receive correspondence at that address. Even better, get the trust a mail drop of its own and thus afford yourself a little extra privacy.

How to Handle Assets: No Commingling

If you mix your personal assets with that of the trust, you could ruin all your plans for privacy. If you receive a check written out to you personally, you must not deposit it in the trust's account. Either cash the check or have the person or organization that wrote the check reissue it to your trust. What's yours is yours, and what's the trust's is the trust's, and never the twain shall meet.

Renting

In general, renting puts your privacy at greater risk. For this reason, I don't recommend renting, although obviously in certain circumstances it is unavoidable. If you must rent, the best way to do it is to have a trust or LLC or IBC rent for you. That way your name is never involved.

In terms of privacy, the biggest problem with renting is that virtually all landlords perform background checks, credit checks, and so on. (This is quite understandable, of course. Landlords have to be careful about the renters they select. For instance, under present laws, if a landlord's tenants are arrested for a drug-related crime involving the rented house, the authorities can simply confiscate the house.) If you're dealing with an individual landlord rather than a property management company and you're willing to offer a large cash deposit, you may have some more luck in protecting your privacy. Similarly, to ensure that your utilities do not give away your identity, you can make an arrangement with the utility companies whereby you submit a large cash deposit.

THE ULTIMATE PRIVACY MOVE

Moving to a new house is the way to really guarantee Third Dimension Privacy. This is a drastic step, of course—one that many are understandably not prepared to take. Nevertheless, it is a way to assure yourself of *total* anonymity. If you simply transfer your house into a trust, someone could still invade your privacy by discovering where you used to live and then determining that you are there as the trust's guest. But if you sell that old house and then have another trust or IBC purchase a new piece of property, you will be much less traceable.[3]

MAIL PRIVACY

We've seen how you don't want to use your real address for anything. It's too much of a threat to your privacy. But what about the mail itself? How do you handle it?

If you have decided to pursue Third Dimension privacy, you need to be able to send and receive mail without fear that it will be tampered with. Plenty of people—identity thieves, petty criminals, and even government agencies—make it their full-time job to snoop through other people's mail. This is one reason, among many, that you don't want to receive mail at your private residence. It is too easy for the bad guys to access your mail and remove or tamper with whatever they want. This is much more difficult if the mail is delivered to a post office box or, preferably, a mail drop. But even then, mail can be intercepted along the way.

While the unauthorized opening of mail is illegal, snoops have various ways of peeking into your mail without actually tearing the envelope. For example, a thief or private detective can use a chemical spray to see through an envelope, and still he has not technically opened your mail. Keep in mind also that the U.S. Postal Service often cooperates with investigating government agencies and that even mail drops have been known to turn over mail to private investigators using a believable pretext.

Thus, in some cases you may wish to make sensitive documents you are sending "snoop proof." The Finland-based company ACL Security has provided several techniques you can use when sending sensitive information through the postal system that will deter potential predators from violating your privacy. Some of these are good commonsense approaches to protecting important material:

- *Bankers' envelopes.* Bankers' envelopes are made from opaque paper and some of them have a pattern on the inside. Holding these envelopes up to a light in order to see through them will not be of any use to someone trying to peek at what you have written.
- *Extra tape.* By using scotch tape you can double seal the entire envelope. As an extra measure of safety, ACL recommends dabbing superglue on the envelope to ensure that the flap isn't loosened.
- *Downplay the address.* When you are sending sensitive information, try to disguise the nature of the recipient so as not to tip off others to the contents. For instance, when sending a letter to a bank or investment broker, you could

PRACTICAL PRIVACY TIP #14:
Buy a Shredder and Use It

Even if you secure a mail drop, what happens when you bring your mail home? If you simply throw the mail away, then anyone—including the trash collector or a private eye—can connect your mail drop with your real address. To get around this, you can buy a shredder. These are quite inexpensive; I bought mine for less than $30.

Make sure you get a "cross-cut" shredder that will process at least five sheets at a time. A cross-cut shredder cuts the paper into little squares, whereas a standard shredder produces long strips, which are easier to reassemble.

I shred the following items before putting them into the trash:

1. Any envelope with my name and/or address on it.
2. Any direct mail advertisement, including preapproved credit card offers, with my name on an interior insert or on the letter itself. (Look carefully: your name and/or address may be buried deep inside the package.)
3. Any catalogs with my name on the front or back cover. I just rip the page off the catalog and shred, throwing the rest of the catalog away as usual. (By the way, this is why you want a shredder that can handle at least five sheets at a time; some of these catalog covers and inserts are thicker than ordinary paper.)
4. Any self-mailer (e.g., a newsletter) with my name and/or address on it.
5. Any bills or statements I've decided to dispose of. (I generally keep these in a file for about twelve months before discarding them.)

If you buy a shredder, make sure members of your family understand this procedure so that they don't inadvertently dispose of anything that hasn't been "processed."

write the name of the person and the street address without mentioning the company.[4]

ACL offers a couple of additional, perhaps drastic, precautionary measures for sending mail. It is, as always, up to you to determine how far you want to go to protect yourself. For those who want the utmost security from mail snoops, ACL gives the option of using a felt-tipped pen or fountain pen to address letters. If chemicals are used in tampering, they will make the ink run. Another possibility is to wrap letters in carbon paper. Chemical tampering will make the carbon run and alert you that someone has been trying to look into your envelopes. Some people go so far as to wrap letters in aluminum foil; that way, if chemicals make the envelope transparent, the snooper still won't be able to read the letter.

CONCLUSION

As we've seen, there are many good reasons why we might want to keep the location of our homes private. You *can* take steps to give yourself and your family more privacy—and consequently more safety—if you really want that protection. It simply comes down to how much convenience you also want.

CHAPTER TEN

MEDICAL RECORDS

*Whatsoever things I see or hear concerning the life of men,
in my attendance on the sick or even apart there from, which
ought not be noised abroad, I will keep silence thereon, counting such things to be as sacred secrets.*

> —Hippocratic Oath (circa fourth century B.C.)

Many people are familiar with the Hippocratic Oath that all doctors must take. Because of that, and because of what we've seen in countless hospital dramas on television, we are inclined to believe that our doctors won't share our personal information with anyone but members of our family—that, when it comes to our medical records, our privacy is protected.

Sadly, that isn't the case.

In fact, in today's society, the sharing of medical information is quite legal. As Georgetown University's Health Privacy Project points out, we all share personal, sensitive information with our doctors, and many different groups can get access to this information. Insurance companies, medical researchers, and pharmacies are just some of those who look at our private medical records.[1]

Consider what happened to psychiatrist Linda Hughes in 1998. Though Dr. Hughes was accustomed to visits from various sales representatives—that's simply the nature of her business— one day a pharmaceutical saleswoman presented information that shocked her. The salesperson handed Dr. Hughes a computer printout of thirty-one patients to whom she had prescribed antidepressants. The printout featured not just the patients' names but also their birth dates and employers.

The salesperson's purpose was simple: she wanted to convince Dr. Hughes that these patients would be better served by her company's drugs than by those currently being prescribed. It didn't matter that those thirty-one patients may not have wanted strangers to know they were receiving psychiatric treatment. Somehow the information had found its way into a database to which the salesperson had access.[2] Amazingly, the pharmaceutical company did nothing illegal to obtain these medical records. *There are no federal laws against sharing medical information.* As for state laws, there are just a few regulations here and there. The *Dallas Morning News* offered this example: "In Texas, health authorities can't disclose the fact that a person has eaten bad oysters. Names in disease outbreaks are confidential. But get a prescription filled for Viagra, and no law keeps it a secret. 'What people have to rely on now is a patchwork of state laws, ethical guidelines that their doctors follow, and luck,' said Janlori Goldman, director of the Health Privacy Project."[3]

In reality, business pressures prevail in the medical industry just as they do in other industries. Information is power.

Companies want your private information in order to manipulate you into purchasing their services. And the system that allows them to collect such information is also available, of course, to private investigators, stalkers, and other individuals who know what they are doing.

CONFIDENTIALITY? YEAH, RIGHT!

Many groups want and can get access to your medical information. These include data clearinghouses, government agencies, insurance agencies, employers, pharmacies, marketers, researchers, the courts, and other patients.[4] As we have seen, no federal laws and, as it turns out, very few state laws exist to protect you. In other words, you are left exposed. Here's how it happens:

- *Data clearinghouses.* The most notable clearinghouse is the Medical Information Bureau (MIB). Its primary job is to provide patient history information to insurance companies, much as the big three credit bureaus provide credit history information to creditors.[5] When you receive health assistance you typically sign a waiver allowing the provider to share the information with anyone who can demonstrate a compelling need for it. This information routinely goes to the MIB. In fact, the waiver often mentions the MIB by name.
- *Government agencies.* A number of government agencies (including the Social Security Administration and Medicare) keep track of people's medical information. They do so to check that individuals are eligible to receive medical benefits.
- *Insurance agencies.* Certainly, an insurance company needs your medical records in order to know when and how much to pay you, so it is not surprising that insurance agencies demand patients' medical information. But they often share

this information quite freely. Insurance companies are not that much different from banks, which sell their customer information to telemarketers, or Web sites like Amazon.com, which regard their database of customers as a corporate asset.

- *Employers.* Medical records are just one of many areas in which employers can be a threat to privacy. When a company provides medical insurance or establishes a fund for employees as a self-insured company, it usually asks its employees to sign an authorization for disclosure of medical records. Whether such information is kept confidential or even stored in a safe place is completely up to the employer.

- *Pharmacies.* Pharmacies see sensitive medical information— the medicine you're taking and, by extension, what you're being treated for. In one case, a pharmacy employee spread the word that a customer was being treated for a venereal disease. The employee was lying, but a judge ruled that there was no privacy violation because the pharmacy owed customers no confidentiality on prescriptions.[6] More commonly, pharmacies use their information about patients to pitch new drugs.

- *Marketers.* Marketers can buy people's medical data from medical brokers, just as they do financial or other demographic data. For instance, pharmaceutical companies have purchased patient prescription records from pharmacies to find target markets for their drugs. Another way they identify potential markets is to offer free "health screenings," such as tests for blood pressure, cholesterol, or body fat. You should thus be cautious about participating in free screenings, especially if your name is attached to the test results. Always assume that the information will be used in the sponsor's marketing programs and sold to third parties.

- *Researchers.* There are federal regulations in place regarding the use of patient information in medical research, but these apply only to federally funded researchers. But more and more research is privately funded, and the federal regulations don't affect this research.[7]

- *Courts.* In certain cases or administrative hearings, such as those involving worker's compensation, courts can subpoena relevant parts of your records—which can become a matter of public record and can even end up in the newspaper.[8]
- *Other patients.* It's human nature to want to talk to other people about health-related issues, to get encouragement and advice from someone who has had the same medical condition. The Internet is a perfect opportunity for this kind of feedback, to find others who have faced or are facing the same situation. But as I advised earlier, use a pseudonym on the Web and avoid filling out information when Web sites ask you to. Remember, anything you discuss about your medical conditions in chat rooms and Usenet groups can be repeated anywhere.

A VAST NETWORK

In truth, the threat to your medical profile is of a piece with the growing invasions into all aspects of your private life. No longer can you be concerned just with a single entity trying to learn about some aspect of your life. As we move into an era of conglomerations that work in a vast array of industries, and as technological advances allow groups to accumulate and access reams of data, your medical information is just part of a comprehensive profile companies can assemble. For example, David Wasson of the *Tampa Tribune* reports:

> Driving the concern is what critics call a gaping loophole in a federal overhaul of financial industry regulations last year. Financial services firms have become increasingly diverse, with many now

having affiliated insurance companies, commercial banks and stock brokerages. Those companies, under the overhaul, are able to share detailed financial and medical profiles of their customers with their affiliates. Privacy advocates worry that consumers could find themselves being denied bank loans not because of their credit histories but because the loan officers had concerns about the applicant's medical profile, which was obtained from an affiliated insurance carrier.[9]

Everything I wrote in Chapter 8 about banking and finances is connected to our medical privacy (or lack thereof). Because of legislation allowing for these sorts of combined services, our privacy can be destroyed as never before. A single company can now construct a database containing comprehensive profiles of people, featuring both financial and medical information—and, very likely, Social Security numbers.

Legislators have proposed bills that would block this sort of privacy invasion, but, so far, they have not passed. The financial services industry, for one, has lobbied vigorously against such legislation.[10]

In short, the unholy union between different financial services and the medical profession demonstrates that the invasion of privacy is a unified assault, as different groups can pool their information about us to develop comprehensive profiles. This network, involving the government and business, also allows criminals to track us in ways never before possible. Our society simply has recognized how easily information can be stored, collated, and transferred.

Fortunately, we can keep our information from becoming public record—our medical profile as well as all our other information.

WHAT IS AT STAKE?

What can happen to us if our medical records are not kept confidential? The U.S. Department of Labor has revealed some frightening examples involving only one aspect of the invasion of privacy—information about one's genetic inheritance:

- A health screening revealed that one man was a carrier of a single mutation for the metabolic disorder Gaucher's disease.[11] Carrier status indicated that he might pass this mutation to his children but not that he would develop Gaucher's disease himself. Nevertheless, he was denied a job when he disclosed his genetic mutation, even though the mutation had no bearing on his present or future ability to perform that or any job.

- A fifty-three-year-old man at a job interview with an insurance company revealed that he had hemochromatosis (a disorder of iron metabolism) but was asymptomatic. During the second interview the company said it was interested in hiring him but would not be able to offer him health insurance due to the genetic condition. He agreed to this arrangement, but during the third interview the company told him that it would like to hire him but could not because of his condition.

- An employee's parent developed Huntington's disease (a neurological disorder that could ultimately lead to dementia)—indicating that the employee had a 50 percent chance of inheriting the mutated gene that causes the disease. A genetic counselor advised the employee to secure life and health insurance before getting tested herself because a positive test result would not only mean that she would get the disease but would probably prevent her from obtaining insurance as well. A coworker overheard her making arrangements to be tested and reported the conversations to their boss. Initially, the boss seemed sympathetic and offered to help, but when the test revealed that the employee did carry the mutated gene, she was fired from her job. (In the eight months prior to her termination, she had received three promotions and outstanding performance reviews.) Frightened by their sister's experience, none of her siblings are willing to undergo genetic testing for fear of losing health insurance or jobs. Consequently, they must live with the uncertainty of not knowing whether they have inherited the gene that leads to Huntington's disease.[12]

Clearly, a lack of medical privacy can cost you a great deal. If your genetic makeup indicates a disease or disability in the future, then you also face the real possibility of losing your means to support yourself in the near term. Moreover, as the story about psychiatrist Linda Hughes indicated, the invasion of our medical privacy means that strangers can learn some of the most intimate details of your life. In the words of the Electronic Privacy Information Center, "Besides information about physical health, these records may include information about family relationships, sexual behavior, substance abuse, and even the private thoughts and feelings that come with psychotherapy."[13]

Medical privacy can involve the most important privacy a person has.

DON'T WAIT FOR A SOLUTION

It would be wonderful if someone would step in and protect us from any invasion of our medical privacy, but that is unlikely to happen. Various groups claim to *need* access to your private information and will make their case to the government, leaving the courts and legislative bodies to resolve these prickly issues. And keep in mind that the government itself is often a threat to our privacy.

For example, the Financial Services Act of 1999 contained a section loudly trumpeting "CONFIDENTIALITY OF HEALTH AND MEDICAL INFORMATION." While this sounds reassuring, the bill stated that there are key exceptions to the confidentiality of our medical records:

- Anyone affiliated with a medical insurer can be given medical records without the consent or knowledge of the person to whom those records refer.
- Records, including personal identifiers, can be given out for "research projects" without the consent or knowledge of the person to whom this information pertains.
- Insurers can give your medical information to credit bureaus.
- Insurers can give your medical information to banks.
- Insurers can give your medical information to debt-settlement entities.
- Insurers can give your medical information to law enforcement without requiring a warrant.[14]

Knowing your rights and then asserting them are the first steps in reclaiming your privacy.

TAKING ACTION

Because your medical information is available to anyone with a bona fide reason to see it—or enough personal initiative to get it—and because this situation is unlikely to change, you must act on your own to protect your medical profile. After all, it is possible that you could be denied a job, a promotion, or insurance coverage because of outdated or erroneous information.

The MIB

The first action to take in regaining your medical privacy is to request your records from the MIB. You can find the organization's Web site at www.mib.com. A copy of your MIB file will cost you $8.50. You can download the documents for U.S. citizens at www.mib.com/consumer/D2.pdf. The MIB does not keep a file on everyone, but if it has one on you, you should get hold of it. Once you have it in hand, you are in a position to clean up erroneous entries.

Other Databases

Regulations vary from state to state, but your health-care provider may be required to give you copies of your medical records. You will probably have to make the request in writing and pay some small fee for making the copies. If you are refused this information, you should contact a patients' advocacy group, a local medical society, the state medical board, or a lawyer.

Be Careful What You Sign

You can stop health-care providers from sending information to the MIB by modifying the standard waiver you are asked to sign before receiving medical attention. A standard waiver might say something like, "I authorize the above-named physician, hospital, or other medical provider to release any information regarding my medical history, symptoms, treatment, exam results, or diagnosis to any party they deem necessary, including the Medical Information Bureau."

Frankly, I believe you should simply cross out entire sections like this and then initial the change. I am not alone in making this recommendation. Janlori Goldman and Zoe Hudson of the Health Privacy Project write that you should read any authorization form before signing in order to see who will receive your medical

records; "you may," they add, "be able to limit distribution and secondary disclosures of the information by revising the authorization
form."[15]

I did this when I increased my life insurance coverage. As part
of the application process, I was treated to a minimal medical
examination in my office. It began with a comprehensive questionnaire about my medical history. I was more than a little
uncomfortable sharing all this information, but I complied to be
certain I received the coverage. When the examiner was done with
her questions, she handed me the form and asked me to sign it.
Reading the fine print, I found that the form included a waiver
granting the insurance company the right to send my information
to the MIB *and* to *anyone* else it cared to.

I crossed out the entire waiver and then printed on the form:
"If the Company transmits any of the Applicant's medical information to a third party, including the MIB, without the Applicant's
prior written consent, the Company will assume liability for any
damages arising therefrom." I initialed the changes, had the examiner do the same, and then made a copy of the form. That was
months ago, and I haven't heard a thing since.

Does this guarantee the privacy of my medical records?
Probably not. But it does provide recourse in the event I need it.

In addition, you can and should use some judgment as to when
some medical information needs to be kept strictly confidential.
For example, if you are concerned about a specific procedure or
condition, you can bring a written notification to your doctor, stating that you revoke any permission you may have given in the past
allowing your information to be shared with third parties and that
you refuse to allow such sharing in the future. You will likely have
to assume full responsibility for any costs related to your treatment, however. Moreover, in certain situations—as one writer

suggests, in cases of highly sensitive disclosures, such as "a consultation that indicates a nervous disorder, a psychiatric problem, or a sexually transmitted disease"[16]—you may want to go to another doctor and pay with cash.[17]

Handling Insurance

As much as we look at employer-provided medical insurance as a benefit, you should note that you are paying a price for such benefits—you are losing some privacy.

One way to help protect your privacy would be to provide your own insurance, if you decide you can afford it. You might work for your company as a contractor, if you can get your employer to agree to it. Then your company won't learn your medical information, and it also doesn't have to record your Social Security number and other facts about you. (You will have to provide a Tax ID number, but this can be your entity ID number rather than your personal Social Security number.) Getting the company to contract with a legal entity like an LLC or a trust affords you another layer of privacy, of course.

If you get insurance under your own name and want to take yet further precautions, you might use some of the "alternative identity" options talked about in Chapter 11. This step will prevent investigators from locating you in such databases as that of the MIB.

CONCLUSION

As with all other facets of privacy, how much medical privacy you can have depends on how badly you want it and how much you are willing to sacrifice.

The first thing to do is get your records and clear up any problems you see in them. You might also try to control the amount of information an insurance company and your doctor's office can give away about you. Ask them not to use your Social Security number. If your Social Security number is on your insurance cards, then photocopy the card with the number blotted out and carry *that* around instead of your card.

Having taken those basic steps, you can begin considering what else you can afford to do to keep your medical life as confidential as possible.

CHAPTER ELEVEN

IDENTIFICATION DOCUMENTS

What a curious phenomenon it is that you can get men to die for the liberty of the world who will not make the little sacrifice that is needed to free themselves from their own individual bondage.

—Bruce Barton (1886–1967)

According to an old adage, "You can tell a lot about a person by the company he keeps." With a little research, it is easy to discover where a person works, who his neighbors are, where he goes to church, what clubs and organizations he belongs to, whom he communicates with on a regular basis, what magazines he subscribes to, and where he vacations. From this data, government agencies, corporate marketers, and even sophisticated criminals can build a profile of you—one that could put you on a suspect list, a prospect list, or a hit list, depending on who's doing the tracking.

Consider the growing threat to our senior citizens, who have been targeted for all sorts of crime. In fact, identity theft has become such a concern for older people that TREA Senior Citizens League, a national organization, has publicly issued warnings about the problem.[1] According to Detective Rick Childress of Ogden, Utah, who investigates financial crimes primarily, elderly persons are a preferred target of identity theft and other crimes of that nature because they tend to be trusting. They also tend to be more fearful about the future and thus are more likely to be lured into a scam designed to elicit their Social Security number or some other piece of confidential and exploitable information. Childress summed it up: "Most of our senior citizens are retired and really want to keep their money safe. Many times all it takes is someone to be nice to them and gain their trust before they steal everything the senior citizen owns. It happens all the time."[2]

How can an elderly person deal with this danger? Frankly, the precautions are the same for the elderly as they are for anyone else. We all need to give out minimal information and always make sure that such information is necessary. As far as phone calls are concerned, Childress provides a good rule: "I wouldn't give out my Social Security number to anyone for any reason over the phone, I don't care who they are."[3]

And if you take the appropriate steps, you can avoid being targeted in the first place.

Again, the decision is ultimately yours as to which, if any, of these options you pursue. Indeed, some steps may sound drastic to certain readers, while other individuals will want to do as much as possible to protect themselves. That is why you must determine what your privacy objectives are and whether you are in a position to take the steps you'd like to take. Always remember that some protection is better than none at all.

SOME BASIC PRECAUTIONS

Before all else, you can take a few basic steps to protect yourself when it comes to your identification documents. One thing you can do immediately is to try and get the Department of Motor Vehicles to issue you a driver's license without your Social Security number printed on it. In my home state, for example, the DMV has a procedure in place for this. All you have to do is check a box in the application to indicate that you do not want your SSN to appear on your license. Many other states have similar procedures.

Another thing you can do is to acquire and use a passport for banking and other purposes. As privacy advocate J. J. Luna points out in *How to Be Invisible*, a passport is superior to a driver's license because it doesn't show your Social Security number or address (or even the state in which you live) and because you cannot easily be traced with your passport number.[4] Of course, you should also try to get your Social Security number removed from your license if it is printed there.

Another step, as discussed in the previous chapter, is to attempt to work for your employer through a legal entity you set up, such as an LLC. That is the only way you can keep from revealing your Social Security number to your place of work. In fact, when your employer hires you he is *required* to get your Social Security number and register you in a federal database of new hires. Furthermore, many employers will do extensive and even intrusive background checks before they hire you. Consider these testimonials given to the National Credit Information Network:

> I have been using NCI for years. The wide range of information available saves me time. I love being able to get a wide variety of information from the same vendor. In my business the fewer vendors I need, the more time I have for my customers.
>
> —Ron H., Myrtle Beach, South Carolina

As a business owner, I need to hire dependable employees. NCI gives me access to credit reports from all three bureaus and I only need one account. It's great. When doing pre-employment screening, I love the ability to obtain driving histories and criminal histories on one simple entry form.

—Thomas W., Cleveland, Ohio

AN OUNCE OF PREVENTION

If you want to go beyond basic precautions, another option to consider is the lawful use of secondary identification and aliases. With these, it is possible to keep your associations private. I will discuss several options, all of which are legal and readily available. It doesn't take much money or effort, but it does take discipline.

For the record, I am not advocating that you do anything illegal. For obvious reasons I am opposed to the use of an alternative identity to commit a crime. But bear in mind also that one of the rationalizations for the abolition of privacy is that privacy allows criminals to get away with victimizing others. Thus, anyone using his privacy in order to hurt others is merely providing evidence for that rationalization and is therefore contributing to the assaults on our privacy. What I am suggesting is that you can use an alternative or "ghost" identity to shield you from potential criminals, from various databases that provide information about you that you wish to remain private, and from the government.

THE FIRST OPTION: THE BEST IDENTITY IS A REAL IDENTITY

If you take many of the precautions recommended in this book, you may well feel no need to create an alternative identity. But even if you want to protect yourself more and yet don't want to go so far as to pursue a ghost identity, you do have another recourse.

Let's say you want to move to a new home and you also want this to be the beginning of a new level of privacy for you and your family. You may not need any identification documents at all, if you have a *trusted* friend or relative sign the new lease, order the utilities and the phones, and get a drop box in his own name. That person can open a bank account that you will run, mailing in the deposits. This individual will be your artificial identity, and he will be all the more convincing because he is not a collection of fictitious documents but rather a real person.

This technique can also be used for a business. If you have a person you trust who will sign documents for you and do what you ask, that person can hold a business in his name for you. This person should be of modest means so that if a lawyer ever tries to find deep pockets to sue, your business won't appear to be an attractive target.

What happens if this person dies while the arrangement is in effect? J. J. Luna suggests in his *How to Be Invisible* that you make the person the sole member of an LLC and have him leave you the LLC in his will.[5] That way you won't lose anything.

The major drawback of a real person, naturally, is that a real person may not be available to cooperate with you to protect your privacy. Or worse, he may suddenly cease to cooperate. You could find yourself in a rather difficult situation if instead of being a shield preventing others from tracking your identity, he simply attaches your house or business to *his* identity. For these reasons, many will want to consider other options.

THE SECOND OPTION: A PSEUDONYM

Many people I have encountered want to take the utmost precautions to protect their privacy. You may be one of these people who feel that they won't have enough protection for themselves and their family if they don't do everything possible.

PRACTICAL PRIVACY TIP #15:
Six Documents You Should *Never* Carry in Your Wallet or Purse

When someone is trying to steal your identity, the first thing he needs is your Social Security number. That's the key to unlocking all sorts of secrets about you. As a result, you should never carry anything in your wallet that has your SSN on it. Nor should you carry documents listing your date of birth, another key identifying factor. Right now, pull out your wallet or purse and purge the following items:

1. **Social Security Card.** Since you have this memorized, there's no reason to carry it with you.

2. **Driver's License.** If your driver's license has your Social Security number on it, go to the Department of Motor Vehicles and get a new one that doesn't display your SSN. Most states will allow you the option of not printing it on your license. If your state won't, you may decide to get a lawyer involved.

3. **Insurance Cards.** If your health-care provider, as mine does, uses your SSN as the ID number, you have two options: (a) request a different ID number and card or (b) make a photocopy of the card, blot out the ID number on the copy, and then make a photocopy of that. Cut this copy to size and carry it in your wallet instead of the original card. When you present this card to your doctor, explain why you are not carrying the original and then quote your SSN from memory.

4. **Birth Certificate.** Very few people carry a copy of their birth certificate. But some do, especially if they don't have a passport. For example, a friend of mine carried his birth certificate in his wallet because he didn't have a passport and often needed to

cross into Canada for work. But as I told my friend, carrying your birth certificate is a big mistake—for an identity thief, a birth certificate is even better than a Social Security number. If you don't have a passport, apply for one now. It reveals far less information about you than even your driver's license, for it displays neither your SSN nor your address.

5. **Voter Registration Card.** If your card has your SSN on it, take it out of your wallet or purse. You use this card only once a year anyway.

6. **Handgun Carry Permit.** My state insists on putting a person's SSN on his carry permit. Therefore, I carry the card on my person (back left pocket) but *not* in my wallet.

By the way, whatever you do, do not carry your identity documents around in a notebook-sized day planner. These planners are too easily forgotten and left behind. I used to make this mistake and have left my planner in all kinds of places. Years ago, for instance, I left it at a restaurant in Florida and had to have it sent to me via overnight mail.

With that in mind, I'll present you with steps you can take to secure an alternative identity. Fictitious identities are perfectly moral. Indeed, some pseudonyms have become quite celebrated in this country. A writer named Samuel Clemens, for instance, became far better known by his pseudonym—Mark Twain. Clemens was not alone, for countless writers have used and do use pen names; no one assumes there is anything suspicious about this practice.

Likewise, there shouldn't be anything suspicious about your using a pseudonym to protect yourself from possible invasions of your privacy.

If you do opt to create another identity, be sure to do two things above all else: First, choose a very common name that won't stand out in any list. Second, don't give your pseudonymous twin your birth date, though you probably want to make him about the same age. You might want to choose a holiday just so it is easily memorized and you won't have any problem rattling off the day, month, and year.

Building an Identity

One easy way to begin developing a secondary identity is through your presence on the Web. With a free, Web-based e-mail server, you can assume a new name and identity online. Later, you might put that pseudonym on one of your alternative street addresses, subscribe to some magazines in the name of this alternative identity, list one of your voice mail phones in his name, or allow him to become a signatory on a bank account.

A different option is to establish your pseudonym's identity at your residence. Why? A major reason is that some credit card companies try to make lists of known drop-box locations. Another benefit is that you can keep your residence private by using a pseudonym—you'll have no worries when you order a pizza, for example.

This process should gradually take on a life of its own. If you can get a credit card company to include this pseudonym as an approved user of one of your cards, then that identity will be able to purchase items and build up his own credit history. He can do this online quite easily, or even in person on occasion if you've practiced the pseudonym's signature. It will be only a matter of time before your alternative identity is offered his own preapproved credit cards. (By the way, this means you *don't* want to prevent your pseudonym from getting junk mail.)

Next, through your business or corporation or LLC you can give this fictional person the right to sign checks. Get utilities put in his name, using a cash deposit rather than identification.

Pseudonymous ID?

In one sense, you will have alternative identification documents simply with a credit card and a utility bill. And it will likely be no problem to get a library card; often that can be done online. Another idea would be to create business cards, which obviously aren't formal proof of identity but which will go a long way in enhancing your pseudonymity. With these forms of identification you should have a great degree of privacy. You should, for example, be able to check into hotels under your pseudonym and make most of your purchases without revealing your profile to watching eyes.

But there are certain limits to what you can do. For this reason, plenty of books have suggested that you build a new identity on forged documents or an acquired Social Security number. I discourage this practice, however. Most of these methods are highly risky at best, and in general they really don't offer much privacy. A new name and new Social Security number can be profiled and tracked just as the old ones were. I'm encouraging paths that will help you live a private life and prevent your identity from being tracked; I'm not urging that you escape from your past and acquire a completely new and fictitious identity.

Another temptation is to augment a pseudonymous identity with fake identification documentation. My advice, however, is to be satisfied with legitimate identification you can acquire for your pseudonym and not go too much further. The risks associated with acquiring and carrying fake ID are just too great. For one thing, while the Internet offers many ways to get fake ID, most of these don't look very convincing. According to Ariza Research, most of the vendors selling fake ID either rip off customers entirely or sell them junk.[6] Privacy author J. J. Luna actually ordered fake IDs from many of these sites and in every case either didn't get anything at all or else received a "grossly inferior product."[7] Finally, you certainly don't want to be caught with fake identification. Even if you aren't hiding anything illicit and are just trying to protect your privacy, authorities will assume that you do have something to hide.

CONCLUSION

With a little time and effort, you can protect your real identity. Start with the simple things and then move to the complex. If possible, get your Social Security number removed from your driver's license. Better yet, use a passport for identification—it reveals far less about you. You may also want to create a legal entity that is different from yourself and use it to interact with your employer and others.

If you wish to go beyond basic precautions, you may want to persuade a friend, a relative, or an attorney to sign legal documents on your behalf. If you want even more privacy—or simply don't want the hassle of involving someone else—you can create a "ghost" identity or alias. So long as you aren't doing this for the purpose of defrauding someone else, it is perfectly ethical and legal.[8] This can be as simple as an alternate e-mail address using a bogus name or as elaborate as establishing a secondary name, mailing address, and phone number. Eventually, this identity will take on a life of its own. Just make sure you don't cross the line and end up on the wrong side of the law. This is why I don't advocate obtaining fake ID.

CHAPTER TWELVE

TELEPHONE AND FAX

The telephone is the greatest nuisance among conveniences,
the greatest convenience among nuisances.

—Robert Staughton Lynd

Here's a question to test your privacy knowledge: can you be convicted and imprisoned on the basis of information obtained through the monitoring of your telephone without a warrant?

The answer is yes, you can—at least in cases involving cordless phones. A few years ago a Texas man, Mr. Varing, suspected that his neighbor, Mr. Smith, had burglarized his house. Varing didn't simply get angry; he attempted to get proof. He used a radio scanner to monitor the calls that Smith made or received on his cordless phone.

Varing did not find any evidence that implicated Smith in the burglary, but he did learn about Smith's drug deals. He informed the police, who then asked him to record the calls. After Varing handed over the tapes to the police, they arrested Smith on narcotics charges.

Smith argued that his arrest was illegal based on the Fourth Amendment (prohibiting unreasonable searches and seizures) as well as the Omnibus Crime and Control and Safe Streets Act of 1968 (a.k.a. the "Wire Statute"). Because the police had directed his neighbor to record his conversations, Smith argued, they were monitoring his phone conversations without a warrant.

But the court decided otherwise. It ruled that violating a person's Fourth Amendment rights requires a significant intrusion on a person's *reasonable* expectation of privacy. Smith, the court said, did not prove that he had a reasonable expectation that his calls on the cordless phone would be private, so there was no reason to believe that his Fourth Amendment rights had been violated. In other words, because the technology of some cordless phones allows anyone nearby to listen in easily, it is not reasonable for people to expect their conversations on such devices to remain private—even though most people expect their phone conversations to be confidential.[1]

Here's a second question: what does a police officer have to do in order to get a list of all the phone numbers you dial?

Unfortunately, unlike what you might think, he doesn't have to show "probable cause" that a crime has been or will be committed to get a warrant. In fact, he doesn't need a warrant at all. All he has to do is get a judge to agree that the phone numbers you dial are "relevant" to an ongoing investigation.[2]

While Congress, at the urging of privacy advocates, has moved to make investigators meet the same requirements for acquiring phone numbers as they do for tapping phones, the Justice Department insists that they should be able to get this sort of information easily, maintaining that "changes would threaten public safety and make it more difficult to find and prosecute criminals."[3] Congressman Mel Watt of North Carolina showed he had a grasp of the principles behind the issue when he responded to the Justice Department by saying, "My Constitution wasn't written for the protection of the prosecutor. For the life of me, I can't see anything in my Constitution that talks about the term 'relevant to an ongoing criminal investigation.' I think what you're trying to do is get the Constitution subcommittee to write a prosecutor standard rather than a Constitution standard."[4]

This sort of privacy nullification is not limited to the United States. In the summer of 2000 a law was passed in England stating that the police no longer have to request a warrant from the Home Secretary if they want to intercept electronic communications and instead can simply go to a police superintendent.[5] Once they secure this easily acquired permission, the police can monitor what is said over a target's mobile phone. In addition, they can track his location as long as his phone is turned on. Caspar Bowden of the Foundation for Information Policy sums up the situation: "Anyone using the new phones will be able to be tracked with pinpoint accuracy at the click of a mouse for very broad purposes. It's like putting an electronic tag on most of the population."[6]

How does this government monitoring work? Simple. It's a standard feature on the new wireless phones. Ostensibly, mobile phone manufacturers developed this technology—the General Packet Radio Service (GPRS) and the Universal Mobile Telecommunications System (UMTS)—for emergency services and to offer location-based services through the mobile Internet. For example, they want to develop services that would allow amateur sailors and bike riders to dial a number and discover their current latitude and longitude. They also envision a "friend finder" that would enable users to know the location of friends who have volunteered to let their cell phones reveal where they are at certain times.[7]

These mobile-positioning technologies are making their way across the Atlantic. The Federal Communications Commission (FCC) successfully pushed for new legislation to make it possible.[8] Associated Press writer Anick Jesdanun describes our near future vividly: "Imagine walking by a Starbucks in an unfamiliar city. Your cell phone rings, and a coupon for coffee pops up on its screen, good only at that location. How did your phone know you were even near that particular Starbucks? What else does it know about you? Enter location tracking, coming to a mobile device near you."[9]

Almar Latour of the *Wall Street Journal* (Interactive Edition) raises some other unsettling possibilities:

> My boss likes to think of mobile phones as umbilical cords that connect his employees to him around the clock. He may be pleased to know that soon he can stick willing underlings in a high-tech womb of sorts and know their whereabouts at all times. That's because of the next wireless thing: mobile positioning. Yes, your mobile phone will serve as a location device as long as it is switched on. The function is due to new wireless technologies and old-fashioned math. Basically, operators can calculate where mobile phone users are based on their relative position to so-called base stations, which transmit mobile-phone signals.[10]

Clearly, as technology progresses, the threats to our privacy only multiply. Indeed, as the cases involving police monitoring reveal, our civil liberties may be at stake as well.

RETURN OF THE PARTY LINE

Most people assume that when they speak on the phone or send a letter, fax, or e-mail, they are communicating in private. Hardly. While this may have been true at one time, communications today more often than not resemble a "party line" where anyone who wants to can listen in with very little effort.

Whether it is the federal government's Echelon system—which digitally monitors every phone call, scanning for keywords and recording suspect conversations[11]—or specialized eavesdropping devices now available commercially, personal communications are rarely private and are often compromised.

Even when we think protections are guaranteed, our privacy is sometimes at risk. For example, the global system for mobile communication (GSM)—which services 65 percent of the world's digital wireless users (including American providers such as Pacific Bell Wireless and Voicestream Wireless)—uses encryption to protect customer privacy ... but with one key exception. Some participating countries, such as those under United Nations sanctions, can't provide encryption, so if a GSM user makes a roaming call to one of these countries the conversation will automatically be unencrypted. Furthermore, GSM does not verify that the base station receiving the signal is indeed the intended destination for the message.

This combination of factors leads to a real problem with wireless privacy, as ZDNet News reported: "Experts said it is possible to build a phony base station that jams the signal from the real base station and forces the cell phone to connect to it. The base station then tells the cell phone, in essence, 'You're in Iraq, don't use encryption,' and the call proceeds unprotected with the false base station relaying information between the real base station and the handset."[12] Thus, the best and most unbeatable encryption system in the world would not make a bit of difference. With this technological trick, it is possible simply to shut off the encryption at the source.

Worse, according to David Wagner, a University of California-Berkeley computer science professor, the experts had identified this loophole long before it became public knowledge.[13] This failure to disclose a threat to users' privacy raises a disturbing possibility: that there are serious privacy breaches that other manufacturers choose not to disclose.

So, as the old saying goes, "Let the buyer beware." Don't simply rely on what the provider tells you about his product and its privacy protections. If you want to ensure your privacy, check with groups that do privacy research—and be certain to take steps on your own to protect yourself.

TAKING ACTION

We've already seen how we can protect our communications through the use of mail drops, various encryption technologies, anonymous browsers, and specific communications protocols. Now it's time to look at how we can guarantee the privacy of phone conversations and fax communications.

Perhaps Low-Tech Is Best

One way to guarantee the privacy of your communications is, of course, not to use the phone or fax. Privacy consultant J. J. Luna goes so far as to advise his readers not to have a phone at all. I don't recommend that extreme recourse. You have other options. But I do recommend that you try as much as possible to reserve sensitive communication for face-to-face conversation. Building the discipline of restraining yourself from using the phone for confidential discussions is an effective way of preserving your privacy. This means that you also have to teach the rest of your family to develop the same discipline. Labels or stickers on your phones might be something you could try. If your whole family is not on board, then you will not be able to protect your privacy.

Cordless Phones

According to privacy author Larry Sontag, "Cordless phones are about the same as yelling out the window."[14] J. J. Luna also discusses the problems with cordless phones:

> ABC television's *Good Morning America* ran a feature about the extreme dangers inherent in the use of cheap cordless phones. Charles Gibson quoted authorities that say sixty-five percent of all Americans have a cordless phone in the house and "ninety percent of all conversations can be listened to." And many are! One unhappy cordless owner, interviewed in shadow, said he was suing the manufacturer, because the instruction booklet said his cordless phone was "secure." He was also suing the dealer, because the salesman confirmed the information that conversations would be secure. Believing what he heard and read, he then used this phone to talk about intimate details of his life with his lawyer, his doctor, and others. When a friend finally confessed to him that neighbors were scanning every conversation—and laughing!—he was so embarrassed that he sold his home and moved away.[15]

In another case, a Georgia chief of police used a scanner to eavesdrop on the cordless phone conversations of his neighbor, a Georgia Bureau of Investigation (GBI) agent. Having listened to his neighbor talk to a former agent about an ongoing GBI investigation, the police chief alerted the subject of the investigation, a city official. The official informed the mayor and the GBI agent's supervisor.[16]

So how should you address the issue of cordless phones? There are some options:

1. *It's best if you don't own a cordless phone.* On older models of cordless phones, conversations can easily be picked up not only by radio scanners but also by baby monitors and similar devices. Newer models are getting better, but it's still unclear how much better they actually are. Why risk privacy for so little convenience? It isn't that hard to get a phone with a long line that will give you some mobility.

2. *If you do own a cordless phone, obtain a second line and hook up a normal (noncordless) phone to it.* Assume you're talking to someone on a normal phone and you have a cordless phone somewhere else in the house hooked up to the same line. Did you know that the base of the cordless phone could still broadcast your conversation even though you are not talking on that particular phone? Newer models are not as prone to this, but it is hard to be certain. If you need to make a truly private call, use the second line.

3. *If you do have to use a line with a cordless phone attached to it, be careful what the other party says.* If the other person starts to reveal some personal information, such as an account number or Social Security number, stop him. Tell him the line is not secure and offer to call back on one that is. It is also essential, of course, to make sure *he* is not talking on a cordless phone (or on a line with a cordless attached to it).

4. *If someone does call you using a cordless phone, be careful what you say.* If you learn the person is using a cordless phone, you should first see if he can pick up a normal phone and disconnect the cordless phone from the line entirely. If he can't

for some reason, you have to be circumspect, knowing that the conversation can easily be scanned.

If this all seems too complicated, return to suggestion number one at the top of the list—that's the best route to take. Actually, if something is really confidential, I don't use the phone at all. I prefer to use encrypted e-mail (see Chapter 7). That way I don't have to worry that the other person is using a cordless phone or that the communication is otherwise compromised on his end. Cordless phones are certainly not the only concern. Cellular phones are also an issue, as we will see. And if you're talking to someone whose phone is tapped, none of your efforts to make sure your line is clear will prevent a third party from listening in.

Again, the most basic precaution is to think about what you say over the phone. Always ask yourself: are you saying something that you are willing for everyone to know?

Cell Phones

Fortunately, most people are turning to digital wireless phones, whose calls are much more difficult to intercept. But plenty of people are still using cellular technology, so even if you don't have one of the phones, you might be called from a cellular phone. And if you use digital wireless, there might be times when you are outside your service area and have to make a call on analog roam, meaning that the conversation could be overheard. Technically, it is illegal to make or import a scanner that doesn't have certain frequencies blocked—the frequencies used by cell phones. But if someone really wants to listen in on a cellular phone conversation, he will probably find a way, even if it means illegally procuring the right scanner. Worse, it seems that cell phones don't use only those blocked frequencies but actually send out accidental second signals that can be scanned. One privacy expert reports that, as a result, he was able to listen in on his wife's cell phone activity using a legal American scanner.[17] Finally, if you often make highly confidential calls on your cell phone, you should consider obtaining a prepaid cell phone. You can often purchase these using your ghost identity or by providing minimal information, so that the information you exchange can't be tracked back to your real identity.

SOME FINAL PRIVACY ARRANGEMENTS

In addition to the general strategies I have outlined above, there are several specific actions you can take to protect your privacy. Many of these are important to protecting the privacy of your residence as well as your actual communications.

Here are some of your options:

- Whenever you make a call that you don't want to become public knowledge, you should neutralize your redial feature. After your call is finished, hang up, then pick up the phone and push one digit, and then hang up again.
- Get "per line caller-ID blocking" so that people don't automatically see your number or your name when you call them. If you order this service you may find that some people will not accept calls from those who have blocked their ID. You can, however, usually disable per line blocking on a call-by-call basis; where I live the code for this is "*82".
- Be aware that, according to an FCC requirement, all toll-free numbers automatically record your number no matter what sort of call blocking you have. (They do this using an older technology called ANI—automatic number identification. To see this in action, call this toll-free number: 800-555-1160. Even if you have call blocking on, the computer

at the other end of the line can read your number.) And of course if someone does capture your phone number he could always use reverse lookup directories available online to find the location of the phone you are using.

- If you are concerned only about First Dimension Privacy (commercial exploitation), get a second phone line installed and use it to make toll-free calls. Keep the ringer turned off. Anyone you want to hear from will use your main line. With this setup you will be able to make toll-free calls without caring that your number is automatically recorded; simply set up a voice-mail box on the second line to answer tele-marketing calls. Using an alternate identity on this line is even better.

- Learn the normal (non-911) phone numbers for local emergency services. When you make 911 emergency calls, your number is automatically captured. If you have gone through the time and effort to keep your residence private, you don't want to compromise that privacy with one phone call. So use these other numbers in case of emergencies rather than 911. You can put the numbers on your phone or, if possible, program them into your phone.

- Use prepaid long-distance cards, especially those cards that don't require any sort of identification or activation. Making long-distance calls with a card does leave an electronic record, so for extra privacy you can buy cards from different companies and make sure that no one company has a record of all your long-distance calling for a given period of time.

- Instead of buying phone service for your residence, simply purchase a digital wireless phone and use it for all of your needs. If you use your secondary address information, you can secure phone service without giving away your privacy.

Because of the quality and convenience of digital wireless, many have found they no longer need a standard phone.

- J. J. Luna has even suggested getting a pager, since wireless phones can be used to identify your location as long as they are turned on. With a pager you can be contacted at any time, but you won't have to keep your phone on. You could avoid using a wireless phone entirely by going to a phone booth and using one of your prepaid cards.

- If you can afford one, consider buying a satellite telephone. These phones are anonymous and can be used many places all over the globe. Originally designed for yachting captains, they use a system of satellites and are small enough to fit in portable carrying cases. These phones can cost thousands of dollars but are coming down in price. If you are interested, you will find many options on the Internet. To protect privacy you would want to acquire this type of phone using a pseudonym.

- Procure encryption technology to make it more difficult to intercept your telephone and fax communications. You can get a free "beta" version of a program called PGPfone, which turns your computer into a secure phone. (According to the Web site, "It uses speech compression and strong cryptography protocols to give you the ability to have a real-time secure telephone conversation via a modem-to-modem connection. It also works across the Internet!"[18]) Many other companies sell cryptography technology for phone and fax, and this may be an option if you can afford it.

CONCLUSION

Telephones and faxes are vulnerable instruments of communication. Your safest course of action lies in being cautious in what you say and whom you call. If you want to be absolutely certain your conversation is private, have it in person. But obviously we can't avoid the phone altogether. The good news is that, as the ways of intercepting phone calls increase, so do the ways of protecting them. The more a market develops for protecting our privacy over the phone, the more we will see innovative solutions to help us keep our conversations confidential.

THE FUTURE IS IN YOUR HANDS

The only thing necessary for the triumph of evil is for good men to do nothing.

—Edmund Burke

I magine this scenario:

A network of satellites sends a positioning signal to a chip implanted beneath your skin. That chip, powered solely by body heat, relays the signal and your body's vital stats to a ground station. The folks manning that ground station, as well as authorized Internet users, can use that information for identifying you, tracking you and monitoring your health.

Sound far-fetched? It's not. As Fox News reported in October 2000, a company named Applied Digital Solutions (ADS) has unveiled a tracking device known as Digital Angel.[1] ADS's device is smaller than a grain of rice. It tracks the host's location by Global Positioning System satellites and monitors his body functions. This information is sent to local tracking stations, where it can be put on the Internet.[2]

In truth, because this technology is in its infancy, we have no idea what it means for the future. But it certainly raises questions about what lies ahead for privacy. We've seen how computers and the Internet have enabled extraordinary invasions of our privacy. As technologies improve, will we be heading to the panopticon, a society of "total surveillance"?

As always, however, the real issue is not so much the technologies themselves but rather how we react to them. Digital Angel could bring great benefits—for instance, the device could detect a heart attack or allow parents to track a kidnapped child.[3] Similarly, many people are fascinated by the possibilities of biometrics—identifying a person based on some unique personal characteristic, such as fingerprints, speech, the retina, or the face. The *Washington Post* reported as early as the summer of 1999 that a Texas bank enabled customers to withdraw money from an ATM simply by having the machine's hidden camera scan their iris.[4] But as convenient as it might be to withdraw money from an ATM without having to carry a bankcard or memorize a password, this technology ensures that a person will no longer have the luxury of being unrecognized. If we reflexively accept the blessings of new technologies without first considering the effects on our privacy, we will become more and more vulnerable.

Rest assured, surveillance technologies will only get better. But that is why the future is in your hands. Only you can decide what your priorities are. Do you want to embrace all the conveniences that computers, the Internet, and other technologies bring you? Or would you rather take action to protect yourself and your family from privacy invasions—ranging from innocuous, but commonplace, telemarketing calls to the much more dangerous problems of identity theft and stalking?

Though it may seem as if the invasion of privacy is now the norm, it doesn't have to be this way. Not if you understand what is at risk and are willing to take action *now* to assert your rights and reclaim your privacy.

Fortunately, taking action does not mean swearing off technology altogether. In fact, the same technologies that make surveillance possible can make privacy and freedom possible again. But you must understand these technologies and put them to good use. No, you don't need to toss the laptop in the garbage, but you do need to know how to set it up for functional privacy, how to prevent Web sites from tracking you, and more. You don't need to avoid the telephone entirely, but you may need to think about what kind of phone line you have set up in your home or what kind of information you might not want to discuss on the phone.

In the end, you must develop a daily way of life that protects and preserves your privacy. You need to reduce your vulnerability to identity thieves, stalkers, credit agencies, corporate spies, and intrusive government. If you don't resist—and encourage other people to resist—you will later wish you had, when it is far too late.

The time to act is now.

A PRIVACY SELF-ASSESSMENT

The following self-assessment is designed to help you determine your current level of privacy. It's not a scientific instrument, but it will give you a good sense of where you are now. You may want to take the assessment now and then try again in a few months—after you have read the book and implemented some of my recommendations.

Please check the first box that comes to mind. This is likely to give you the most accurate picture of your situation. If you don't know the answer to a question, check "Yes." We are not looking for absolute answers, just general trends. At the end of the assessment I provide a way to score yourself.

PERSONAL INFORMATION

1. When asked for my address, I usually give my residential address. ☐ Yes ☐ No

2. When asked for my phone number, I usually give my residential number.   ❏ Yes   ❏ No

3. When asked for my Social Security number, I usually provide it.
                                                        ❏ Yes   ❏ No

4. When asked for my e-mail address, I offer the only one I have.
                                                        ❏ Yes   ❏ No

5. I throw sensitive information in the trash, including bank statements, credit card statements, and so on.   ❏ Yes   ❏ No

PHYSICAL ADDRESS
6. I receive mail at my home.

                                                        ❏ Yes   ❏ No

7. I receive other deliveries at my home.

                                                        ❏ Yes   ❏ No

8. My utilities are listed in my own name.

                                                        ❏ Yes   ❏ No

9. My home is titled in my own name.

                                                        ❏ Yes   ❏ No

10. I have a mortgage in my own name.

                                                        ❏ Yes   ❏ No

PHONE USE
11. I don't have caller ID.

                                                        ❏ Yes   ❏ No

12. I don't have "per line caller ID blocking."*

                                                        ❏ Yes   ❏ No

---

* This keeps your phone number from being revealed to those you call.

13. I occasionally give out my credit card numbers over a cordless phone.   ❑ Yes   ❑ No

14. I own and use a cordless phone.

❑ Yes   ❑ No

15. My phone is listed in my own name.

❑ Yes   ❑ No

COMPUTER AND INTERNET USE

16. I have only one e-mail address.

❑ Yes   ❑ No

17. My browser is set to accept cookies.

❑ Yes   ❑ No

18. I have not cleared the history on my browser in the past thirty days.   ❑ Yes   ❑ No

19. I do not use a cable lock or other device to protect my computer from theft.   ❑ Yes   ❑ No

20. I do not use a screensaver password.

❑ Yes   ❑ No

21. I use the same password for most applications.

❑ Yes   ❑ No

22. My password is a common word that can be found in the dictionary.   ❑ Yes   ❑ No

23. I do not use an antivirus program.

❑ Yes   ❑ No

24. I do not regularly update my virus definitions.

❑ Yes   ❑ No

25. I occasionally include account numbers or other sensitive information in my e-mails.   ☐ Yes ☐ No

26. I do not use a personal firewall with my Internet connection.   ☐ Yes ☐ No

27. I assume that when I delete files from my computer they are gone.   ☐ Yes ☐ No

PERSONAL FINANCES

28. My bank accounts are in my own name.   ☐ Yes ☐ No

29. My credit cards are in my own name.   ☐ Yes ☐ No

30. I rarely use cash in my financial transactions.   ☐ Yes ☐ No

31. One company provides most of my financial services.   ☐ Yes ☐ No

32. I make regular use of retail discount cards.   ☐ Yes ☐ No

33. I have never considered offshore banking.   ☐ Yes ☐ No

34. I have not requested a copy of my credit report in the past year.   ☐ Yes ☐ No

MISCELLANEOUS

35. I have never requested my medical records from the Medical Information Bureau (MIB).   ☐ Yes ☐ No

36. I generally sign any medical paperwork that is put in front of me without protest.   ☐ Yes ☐ No

37. I always carry my Social Security card in my wallet or purse.
                                                                    ☐ Yes ☐ No

38. My driver's license has my Social Security number printed on it.   ☐ Yes ☐ No

39. I generally use my driver's license for identification purposes.
                                                                    ☐ Yes ☐ No

40. I have been cited for a moving traffic violation in the past year.
                                                                    ☐ Yes ☐ No

SCORING YOURSELF

This is a simple assessment. I make no pretense that it is scientific. Simply count the number of questions to which you answered "Yes." This is your point total. Once you have your total, consult the chart on the following page to see where you stand.

If you scored ...	You are ...
1–10	*A "ghost."* You are essentially invisible to everyone except your family and closest friends. You obviously have a good grasp of privacy issues and have taken significant steps to reduce your risk.
11–20	*Reasonably private.* You understand some of the issues related to privacy and have demonstrated your willingness to do something about it. You have made it difficult for all but the truly committed to find you. With a little extra effort you can move to the next level.
21–30	*Unnecessarily exposed.* You have some privacy, but you are not as careful as you should be. You need to take steps now to shore up your privacy while you still can.
31–40	*Completely exposed.* It's only a matter of time before your lack of privacy catches up with you. You are the ideal target for exploitation.

THE COMPLETE PRIVACY CHECKLIST

H ere's a summary of what you can do. Note that you do not have to do everything on this list. It is up to you to decide how much privacy you want and in what areas.

GETTING STARTED

❑ Read everything about privacy you can get your hands on (see Appendix C).

❑ Discuss privacy issues with your family and review what habits you will all need to develop (see Appendix D).

❑ Arrange for any checks the government sends you to be deposited electronically (so there's less chance that anyone will see your Social Security number).

❑ Find out how your employer stores and secures your private information and who is allowed access to it. Inform your employer if the procedures are not adequate.

❏ Regularly "ego-surf" on the Internet to find out if your privacy is being breached by a cyberstalker.

❏ See if you can get your Social Security number removed from your insurance cards. If not, or until it is removed, photocopy the cards and black out the number; carry the photocopy.

❏ Do not participate in surveys, whether private or government, that ask you to provide personal information such as name, family size, or date of birth.

❏ When information is requested for goods and services, always ask what the information is for, how securely it is stored, who will have access to it, and what will happen to it when it has served its purpose. You may want to begin using the Public Servant Questionnaire (see Appendix E).

❏ Establish an alternative identity on the Internet and wherever else you can.

COMPUTERS AND INTERNET

❏ Put a note on your computers reminding you that e-mail is not private. Be careful what you send.

❏ Sign up for at least one Web-based e-mail service without revealing any of your private information.

❏ Get an ad filter that will keep a banner company from profiling you (see Junkbusters.com).

❏ Disable cookies, or else download a program from CNET.com or ZDNet.com that will "crunch your cookies."

❏ Disable ActiveX, or at least be very cautious with it.

❏ Begin using computer encryption for sensitive e-mails (e.g., Hushmail.com).

❏ Buy a cable lock to make your computer more difficult to steal.

❏ Use your computer's password features.

❑ Download DesktopShield 2000 or some other program that will protect your computer with a better password system.

❑ Make sure your passwords are complex and contain a mixture of letters, numbers, and punctuation marks.

❑ Install a good antivirus program and make sure you keep the definitions updated.

❑ Download a program that will truly wipe old data off your hard drive.

BANKING AND FINANCES

❑ Get a credit report from one of the three credit agencies every year on a rotating basis.

❑ Change passwords to something less obvious than your mother's maiden name.

❑ Operate on a cash basis as much as you can.

❑ Purchase from retailers, using cash, instead of ordering products directly, using a credit card.

❑ Avoid retailers' discount card programs.

❑ Use money orders instead of checks for maximum privacy.

❑ Don't get all your financial services from one institution. Spread yourself out so that no one compiles a profile of you.

❑ Get a pseudonym and add it to those who may use one of your credit cards. Build up a credit rating for this alternative identity.

❑ Form a Limited Liability Company (LLC). If necessary, form several and use them as the need arises.

❑ Decide how you can best divide up your assets and transfer (or exchange) ownership to trusts, International Business Corporations (IBCs), or some other entity.

❑ Move some of your assets to other countries.

❑ Get an offshore credit and/or debit card.

YOUR PHYSICAL ADDRESS

❑ Get a private mail drop and stop receiving mail at your home address.

❑ Develop protective mailing habits.

❑ Use a remailing service or always send mail from a public drop box, using a post office or mail drop as the return address.

❑ Get utilities in someone else's name, in the name of an entity, or with a cash deposit to avoid giving private information.

❑ Have an LLC, a trust, an IBC, or some other entity acquire your primary residence.

❑ Develop the discipline of not speaking of your property as *your* property. Remember: it belongs to the entity that owns it.

❑ Refuse any mail that comes to your home in your own name.

❑ If you rent, get privacy agreements with the landlord in writing and pay the landlord for all utilities.

MEDICAL RECORDS

❑ Contact the Medical Information Bureau (MIB) and get a copy of your records; inform the MIB of inaccuracies.

❑ Get copies of your records from your insurance company and your physicians in order to verify them.

❑ Do not sign a general waiver for the release of information; sign a more specific one, crossing out anything that makes you uncomfortable.

❑ Do not participate in any health screenings that ask for your personal information.

❑ Make sure your health insurance and life insurance come from companies different from those that provide your other financial services.

❑ If you have insurance through your employer, consider seeing a different doctor, and paying in cash, for examinations or treatments you wish to keep confidential.

❑ If possible, get your own insurance and pay most of your doctor bills in cash.

IDENTIFICATION DOCUMENTS

❑ Get your Social Security number off your driver's license.

❑ Get a passport to use as identification rather than a driver's license.

❑ Consider having a trusted relative or friend own things on your behalf; let this person's documents become, in a sense, your identification documents.

❑ Build up a credit rating for an alternative identity and gradually acquire more documentation for him.

❑ For limited identification purposes, consider some forms of alternative identification.

❑ For limited identification purposes, memorize an alternative Social Security number.

TELEPHONE AND FAX

❑ Get rid of your cordless phone or disconnect it whenever sensitive information is passed over the line. (If you're talking to someone on a normal phone but have a cordless phone hooked up to the same line, the base of the cordless phone could still broadcast your conversation even though you are not talking on that particular phone.) If necessary, install a second line with no cordless attached.

❑ Practice asking the other party in a phone conversation what sort of phone he or she is using.

❑ Find out the normal numbers of emergency services (i.e., the non-911 numbers) and post them on your phones or program them in. (Calling 911 will give away your phone number.)

❑ Use a digital wireless phone (preferably bought in a way that hides your identity).

❏ Get a pager and give out this number. Turn on your wireless digital phone only to make outgoing calls.

❏ Acquire and keep on hand a few prepaid long-distance calling cards from different companies.

A COMPREHENSIVE PRIVACY RESOURCE LIST

I n my pursuit of privacy, I have found the following resources helpful. You can find links to most of these resources on my Web site at www.moreprivacy.com.

BOOKS

Anonymous. *New ID in America: How to Create a Foolproof New Identity*. Boulder, CO: Paladin Press, 1983.

Benson, Ragnar. *Acquiring New ID: How to Easily Use the Latest Computer Technology to Drop Out, Start Over, and Get on with Your Life*. Boulder, CO: Paladin Press, 1996.

Charrett, Sheldon. *Identity, Privacy, and Personal Freedom: Big Brother and the New Resistance*. Boulder, CO: Paladin Press, 1999.

———. *The Modern Identity Changer: How to Create a New Identity for Privacy and Personal Freedom*. Boulder, CO: Paladin Press, 1997.

Cornez, Arnold, *The Offshore Money Book: How to Move Assets Offshore for Privacy, Protection, and Tax Advantage*. New York: Contemporary Books, 1998.

Davidson, James Dale, and Lord William Rees-Mogg. *The Sovereign Individual: How to Survive and Thrive During the Collapse of the Welfare State*. New York: Simon and Schuster, 1997.

Givens, Beth. *The Privacy Rights Handbook*. New York: Avon Books, 1997.

Luger, Jack. *Counterfeit ID Made Easy*. Port Townsend, WA: Loompanics Unlimited, 1990.

Luna, J. J. *How to Be Invisible: A Step-by-Step Guide to Protecting Your Assets, Your Identity, and Your Life*. New York: St. Martin's Press, 2000.

Neal, Terry L. *The Offshore Advantage*. Portland, OR: MasterMedia Publishing Group, 1998.

Party, Boston T. *Bulletproof Privacy: How to Live Hidden, Happy, and Free*. Austin, TX: Javelin Press, 1997.

Postman, Neil. *Technopoly: The Surrender of Culture to Technology*. New York: Vintage Books, 1993.

Reid, Barry. *ID by Mail*. Fountain Valley, CA: Eden Press, 1999.

————. *The Paper Trip III: The Master Guide to New Identity*. Fountain Valley, CA: Eden Press, 1998.

Sands, Trent. *Reborn in the U.S.A.: Personal Privacy Through a New Identity*. Port Townsend, WA: Loompanics Unlimited, 1998.

Sontag, Larry. *Privacy: It's None of Your Business*. Seattle: Peanut Butter Publishing, 1998.

WHITE PAPERS AND ARTICLES

Douglas, Robert, President of American Privacy Consultants. "Establishing a Commission for the Comprehensive Study of

Privacy Protection." Testimony before the Subcommittee on Government Management, Information, and Technology of the Committee on Government Reform, U.S. House of Representatives, 12 April 2000. Available online at <http://www.privacytoday.com/HGR04122000.htm>.

————. "Identity Theft and Related Privacy Issues." Testimony before the Committee on Banking and Financial Services, U.S. House of Representatives, 13 September 2000. Available online at <http://www.privacytoday.com/bankingtestimony2000.htm>.

————. "Is It Any of Your Business? Consumer Information, Privacy, and the Financial Services Industry." Statement before the Interagency Public Forum, hosted by the Federal Deposit Insurance Corporation, 23 March 2000. Available online at <http://www.privacytoday.com/FDIC.htm>.

————. "The Use of Deceptive Practices to Gain Access to Personal Financial Information." Statement before the Committee on Banking and Financial Services, U.S. House of Representatives, 28 July 1998. Available online at <http://www.privacytoday.com/bankingtestimony-98.htm>.

Nestman, Mark. "13 Ways to Protect What's Left of Your Privacy and Property Rights." You get this report as a bonus when you sign up for the free Sovereign Society e-mail newsletter (see below, *E-Newsletters*).

Penenberg, Adam L. "The End of Privacy." *Forbes* (29 November 1999). Available online at <http://www.forbes.com/forbes/99/1129/6413182a.htm>.

Poole, Patrick S. "Echelon: America's Secret Global Surveillance Network." Available online at <http://fly.hiwaay.net/~pspoole/echelon.html>.

E-NEWSLETTERS

Offshore & Privacy Secrets. Published by the Offshore Privacy Club. You can sign up at <http://www.offshoreprofit.com/home.html>. I also highly recommend joining the Offshore Privacy Club. You can sign up at the club's Web site.

The Sovereign Society Offshore A-Letter. A free e-mail newsletter published by the Sovereign Society. You can sign up at <http://www.sovereignsociety.com/free.html>. This is a great way to stay on top of the latest privacy and offshore news. Back issues are available at <http://www.sovereignsociety.com/a-letter/index.html>.

DISCUSSION GROUPS

MorePrivacy.com: <http://pub11.ezboard.com/bmoreprivacy>. This is my own message board.

The Sovereign Society Forum: <http://www.sovereignsociety.com/sovboard/index.html>.

NEWS SOURCES

Electronic Privacy Information Center (EPIC): <http://www.epic.org>. Note also the other resources made available on this site.

Privacy Times: <http://www.privacytimes.com>.

Privacy Today News: <http://www.privacytoday.com/headlines.htm>.

WorldNetDaily: <http://www.worldnetdaily.com>. This site runs regular columns on privacy under the column heading "Your Papers Please." The site has hundreds of articles, and you should check back regularly for the latest.

Zero Knowledge Systems' Freedom Web site: <http://www.freedom.net/resources/index.html>.

MISCELLANEOUS WEB SITES
General

Andre Bacard's Privacy Page: <http://www.andrebacard.com/privacy.html>.

Financial Privacy Consultants: <http://financial-privacy-consultants.cx>.

MorePrivacy.com: <http://www.moreprivacy.com>.

Privacy: World's Greatest Links: <http://www.thecodex.com/c_links.html>.

Privacy, Inc.: <http://www.privacyinc.com>.

The Privacy Page: <http://www.privacy.org>.

The PT Club: <http://www.ptclub.com>.

The Sovereign Society: <http://www.sovereignsociety.com>.

Spy World: <http://www.spyworld.com>.

Banking

Privacy Headquarters:
<http://www.privacyheadquarters.com>.

Prosper International League Ltd. (PILL):
<http://www.bankingoffshore.com/pill/28083>.

Fake ID

Fake ID Kit Center: <http://newid.ultramailweb.com>.

NIC Law Enforcement Center: <http://www.nic-inc.com>.

Internet Privacy

Aliro: <http://www.aliroo.com>.

Anonymous News Group Access: <http://www.worldnet-news.com>.

Anti-theft Computer Superstore:
<http://www.galaxymall.com/computer/antitheft>.

Compelson Labs: <http://www.compelson.com/products.htm>.

Computer Security Products:
<http://www.computersecurity.com/laptop>.

Diceware Passphrase: <http://world.std.com/~reinhold/diceware.html>.

Disk and File Shredders: <http://world.std.com/~reinhold/diceware.html>.

EPIC: <http://www.epic.org>.

Evidence Eliminator: <http://www.evidence-eliminator.com/main.shtml>.

Freedom: <http://www.freedom.net>.

Gibson Research Corporation: <http://grc.com/default.htm>. Check out the Shields UP! program.

IBM Security Kits: <http://www.usecure.com/ibm_security_kits.htm>.

Infraworks: <http://www.infraworks.com>.

Internet Privacy Coalition: <http://www.epic.org/crypto>.

Mach5 Enterprises: <http://www.mach5.com>.

NetZero Free ISP: <http://www.netzero.com>. Use a pseudonym to get an anonymous account.

PGP—Home Page: <http://www.pgp.com>.

PGP—International Home Page: <http://www.pgpi.org>.

PGP—MIT Distribution Center: <http://web.mit.edu/network/pgp.html>.

PrivacyMaker: <http://www.privacymaker.com>.

Privacy Software Corporation: <http://www.privsoft.com>.

ProxyJudge: <http://towerofbabel.virtualave.net/cgi-bin/proxjudge.cgi>.

ScramDisk: <http://www.scramdisk.clara.net>.

SecureDrive: <http://www.stack.nl/~galactus/remailers/securedrive.html>.

Shredder: <http://www.gale-force.com/shredder95/indexa.html>.

StealthyGuest: <http://www.stealthyguest.com>.

Ultimate Anonymity: <http://www.ultimate-anonymity.com>.

Webroot Software: <http://www.webroot.com/prod1.htm>.

Wintracks: <http://bv0.free.fr>.

WorldNet News—Privacy Software: <http://www.worldnet-news.com/software.htm>.

Zero-Knowledge Systems: <http://www.zeroknowledge.com>.

ZipLip: <https://www.ziplip.com/zlplus/home.jsp>.

Zone Labs: <http://www.zonelabs.com>.

Mail Drops

Antigua Mail Drop: <http://www.mailantigua.com/about.htm>.

AYOC: <http://www.maildropnet.com>.

Curzon Privacy Services: <http://www.curzoninc.com>.

EscapeArtist: <http://www.escapeartist.com/global/maildrops.htm>.

FINOR: <http://www.finor.com/en/remailing_telephone_fax_email.htm>.

Offshore Mail-Drop Services: <http://www.offshoresecrets.com/maildrop.htm>.

Servcorp Virtual Office: <http://www.cohq.net/site/about_us.html>.

Medical

For the Record: <http://www.nap.edu/readingroom/books/for>.

Medical Record Privacy: <http://www.epic.org/privacy/medical>.

Medical Records, Privacy, and Confidentiality: <http://www.netreach.net/~wmanning/privacy.htm>.

Medical Records Privacy Resource:
<http://wings.buffalo.edu/faculty/research/bioethics/privacy.html>.

Offshore
FINOR Offshore: <http://www.finor.com/index.html>.
Offshore Advantage: <http://www.offshoreadvantage.com>.
Offshore Privacy Club: <http://www.offshore-privacy.com>.
Offshore Secrets: <http://www.offshoresecrets.com>.

Shopping Cards
CASPIAN (Consumers Against Supermarket Privacy
Invasion and Numbering): <http://www.nocards.org>.

Spyware
ASAP Investigations:
<http://www.asapinvestigations.com/frameset.htm>.
A1 Trace: <http://www.a1trace.com>.
Docusearch: <http://www.docusearch.com>.
TR Information Services: <http://www.shadow.net/~trinfo>.
USSearch: <http://www.1800ussearch.com>.

ESTABLISHING A PRIVACY POLICY
FOR YOUR FAMILY

Y ou will not be successful in reclaiming and maintaining your privacy unless the whole family is involved. Therefore, you might want to hold a family meeting and agree on the following privacy policy.

Preamble: We place a high value on protecting our privacy. Every time we lose some of our privacy, we lose some of our freedom. Therefore, we believe that maintaining our privacy is the responsibility of everyone in this home. We understand that this is often inconvenient and expensive. Nevertheless, we are willing to pay the price to preserve it. To do so, we agree to observe the following rules:

1. We don't carry our Social Security card or any document containing our Social Security number on our person.

All a thief needs to steal our identity is our Social Security number. Therefore, we protect this number as though it were the key to all our other possessions.

2. We never provide our Social Security number to another party without challenging the request. Many people will simply drop the request if we refuse to provide our number. In challenging the request, we are willing to make three attempts:

Attempt #1: "I'm sorry, but I have a policy against providing my Social Security number." If the person still insists ...

Attempt #2: "I know you are just doing your job, but I am concerned about identity theft. As you probably know, it always begins with unauthorized access to someone else's Social Security number." If the person still insists ...

Attempt #3: "Okay, may I please speak with your supervisor?" We then need to start over with *Attempt #1*.

Finally, if the supervisor is still insistent, we must find out if we can get this same service or product from someone else. If we can't, then we reluctantly provide the number or forgo the service or product. Even if we provide the number, we say, "Okay, you're not giving me any choice here, so I'm going to give you the number. However, if I find that you have provided this number to anyone else, I will hold you and your company responsible for any damages I incur. Do you understand?"

3. We don't give out our address, phone number, or other personal information to people we don't know and trust. If necessary, we use our "ghost" information. Under no circumstances do we ever associate our real name with our real address or real phone number. (For example, if we want to have pizza delivered to our home, we should use our real address but use an alias. We will be able to do this only if we pay in cash.)

4. We always use passwords, and we change them often. We never use "password" as our password. We try to include a made-up word or a combination of letters and numbers. We store our password in a special encrypted password program. (Consider either Password Officer or the online password storage site steganos.com. The latter is anonymous, free, and fully encrypted.)

5. We don't respond to surveys, questionnaires, or polls— even when they appear to be anonymous. These devices are often deceptive and contain mechanisms for tracking the information back to us. Then, through the use of sophisticated databases, it is collected into comprehensive "profiles" about our interests, affiliations, habits, assets, liabilities, personal history, and so on.

6. We don't participate in preferred customer programs or supermarket discount card programs. The only purpose of these programs is to gather personal information about us or track our buying habits. No matter what the discount incentive is, the price is too high in terms of the privacy we lose.

7. We don't include sensitive information in e-mails. Sending an e-mail is about as private as sending a postcard through the mail. It can be easily intercepted and the information abused. If we do use e-mail, we use encryption technologies.

8. We never respond to spam or junk mail. By doing so, we only confirm our interest in the subject and the validity of the information the sender already has. We simply delete these messages or throw away the unwanted mail. Since we are using a ghost e-mail address and a ghost residential address, we can change it when we grow weary of receiving unwanted solicitations.

9. We never sign digital signature tablets. It's one thing to provide a signature on a piece of paper (like a real credit card receipt). It's quite another thing to let a computer capture our signature. Once our signature is stored digitally, we lose control of it. It can be bought or sold just like any other piece of data.

10. In refusing to provide information, we are always polite but firm. We could say, "I'm sorry, but I (we) have a policy against providing that information." But we also see this as an opportunity to make other people aware of privacy issues. It's not just that we are stubborn or grumpy; instead, we believe something very valuable is at stake. Therefore, we add, "We see it as an invasion of our privacy and would be grateful for your understanding and cooperation."

APPENDIX E
PUBLIC SERVANT QUESTIONNAIRE

F inally, there's a way to turn the tables on those annoying surveys and pollsters. When some government organization wants to survey you, just say, "I'd be happy to consider participating in your survey (questionnaire/investigation/poll). But before I can, I need to ask you a few questions. I have a brief questionnaire that I'd like for you to answer. It will only take about five minutes. Is that okay?"

Then give the questioner the "Public Servant Questionnaire" (PSQ) below. (You can also download a one-page copy of the PSQ from my Web site at www.moreprivacy.com; the downloadable version looks *exactly* like an official government form.) If the person refuses, simply respond, "Well, I'm sorry. Then I won't be able to participate in your survey (questionnaire/investigation/poll) either." And if the questioner agrees to fill out the PSQ, it's a great way to show how you and I feel when we face intrusive questioning.

Public Law 93–579 states in part: "The purpose of this Act is to provide certain safeguards for an individual against invasion of personal privacy requiring Federal agencies and others ... to permit an individual to determine what records pertaining to him are collected, maintained, used, or disseminated by such agencies...." The following questions are based on that Act and are necessary for this individual to make a reasonable determination concerning divulgence of information to this agency.

Name of Public Servant	Proof of Identification (ID No., Badge No., etc.)		
Residence Address	City	State	Zip

Name of department of government, bureau, or agency by which public servant is employed.	Supervisor's name

Office Address	City	State	Zip

Will public servant uphold the Constitution of the United States of America? ❏ Yes ❏ No	Will public servant furnish a copy of the law or regulation which authorizes this survey? ❏ Yes ❏ No
Will public servant read aloud that portion of the law authorizing the questions he will ask? ❏ Yes ❏ No	The citizen's answers are ❏ Voluntary ❏ Mandatory

The questions asked are
❏ Based on a specific law or regulation
❏ Being used as a part of a discovery process

What other uses may be made of this information?

What other agencies may have access to this information?

What will be the effect on the citizen if he chooses not to answer part or all of the questions?

Name of the person in government requesting that this survey or investigation be made:	Does public servant reasonably anticipate either a civil or criminal action will be initiated or pursued based on any information which is sought? ❏ Yes ❏ No

This survey or investigation is (please see note):	Note: The term "General" refers to a blanket survey or investigation in which a number of persons are involved because of geography, type of business, sex, religion, race, schooling, income, etc. The term "Special" refers to a survey or investigation of an individual in which others are not involved.
☐ General ☐ Special	

Is there a file of records, information, or correspondence relating to this citizen being maintained by this agency? ☐ Yes ☐ No	Has public servant consulted, questioned, interviewed, or received information from any third-party relative to this citizen? ☐ Yes ☐ No

If yes, identify all such third parties.

Is this agency using any information pertaining to the citizen which was supplied by another agency or government source? ☐ Yes ☐ No

If yes, which agencies or sources?

Will public servant guarantee that the information collected in this survey or investigation will not be used by any other agency other than the one by whom he is employed? ☐ Yes ☐ No

AFFIRMATION BY PUBLIC SERVANT

I swear (or affirm) under penalty of perjury that the answers I have given to the forgoing questions are complete and correct in every particular. (Please sign in ink.)	Date
First Witness	Date
Second Witness	Date

Please return this questionnaire to the citizen who distributed it. Please allow 4–6 weeks for a response. Filling out and returning this questionnaire is not a guarantee that citizen will participate in agency's survey or investigation. However, no consideration will be given unless this questionnaire is filled out in its entirety and promptly returned.

ACKNOWLEDGMENTS

Because I am professionally involved in the publishing business, every day I am able to witness the incredible number of people it takes to get any book into print and into the hands of readers. What is true in general is especially true with this book.

First, I'd like to thank my wife, Gail, who has put up with me for more than two decades. She and our five daughters have been a constant source of encouragement and patience. I can always count on them to believe in me when I'm not sure I believe in myself.

I'd also like to thank David Dunham, my business partner. He and I learned together about the importance of privacy. He was— and still is—my day-to-day sounding board. As a true friend, he helps me sort out the good ideas from the bad.

My colleagues at Thomas Nelson have always been more than mere associates. They are also my friends and fellow laborers in a calling that gives our lives meaning and purpose. For fear that I would overlook someone important, I won't mention them by name, but you know who you are.

I am grateful beyond words for Mark Horne's assistance with both the research and the writing of this book. Without his help, this project would never have gotten off the ground. He got up to speed quickly and gave shape and momentum to this project.

I would be remiss if I didn't mention my friends at Regnery Publishing: Alfred Regnery, Marji Ross, Harry Crocker, and Jed Donahue provided the necessary expertise to take this project to the next level. Harry and Jed especially helped me to organize my thoughts and clarify my thinking. They were ruthless with the red pencil, but this book is much more readable—and I hope helpful— as a result.

I was first exposed to privacy issues when I spoke at the Global Prosperity conferences. Although I was paid to speak, I was the one who received the education. Other privacy advocates helped along the way with my education, including Katherine Albrecht, Lee Larrison, Bobby Philips, Stan Pierchoski, Dennis and Patty Poseley, Ed and Liberty Rivera, and Franklin Sanders. Grateful acknowledgment is made to those who granted permission to reprint material; my apologies if I've inadvertently overlooked anyone.

I'd also like to thank Sandy Callender, my publicist. As she has taught me, when you've finished writing a book, you're only half done. It is only then that the real work begins—getting people to actually buy the book and read it. Without her tireless efforts, the book you are reading would be in the Regnery warehouse.

NOTES

INTRODUCTION

1. Ralph Jimenez, "Bill Would Ban Raids on Rx Records," *Boston Globe*, 14 June 1998, 1.

2. "Pollsters Access Unlisted Number," *Edmonton Sun*, 18 February 2001, 19.

3. See, for example, "Big Brother Is Watching Us All," *Tampa Tribune*, 18 February 1996, 6.

4. Nina Bernstein, "Lives on File: The Erosion of Privacy," *New York Times*, 12 June 1997, A1.

5. "Technique Forum: Avoid the Internet Rip-off," *Computing*, 1 June 2000, 44.

6. Miguel Helft, "The Real Victims of Fraud," *The Industry Standard*, 6 March 2000.

7. Dorothy Korber, "ID Theft: Tiger's Plight Common," *Sacramento Bee*, 20 December 2000, A1.

8. Dana Hawkins and Margaret Mannix, "Privacy Is Under Siege at Work, at Home, and Online," *U.S. News & World Report*, 2 October 2000, 62; Kelly Flaherty, "Litigation Privilege vs. Privacy Is Issue in Suit," *Recorder*, 9 April 1999, 2.

9. Daniel Weintraub, "Driver's License Fraud—The Victim's Nightmare," *Sacramento Bee*, B7.

10. Amanda Garrett, "Secret Life of a Stalker," *Cleveland Plain Dealer*, 14 July 2000, 1A.

11. Monica Soto, "Kozmo Revises Consent Form," *Seattle Times*, 22 July 2000, B1; P. J. Huffstutter and Robin Fields, "Drug Tests Are Multiple Choice at Tech Firms," *Los Angeles Times*, 2 October 2000, C1.

12. Robert Trigaux, "Cameras Scanned Fans for Criminals," *St. Petersburg Times*, 31 January 2001 <http://www.sptimes.com/News/013101/TampaBay/Cameras_scanned_fans_.shtml> (28 February 2001).

13. I will occasionally recommend specific products or services to help you in the battle to protect your privacy. For the record, I have no financial interest in any of the products or services I recommend.

CHAPTER ONE

1. Stepfather's testimony as published on the AmyBoyer.org Web site: <http://www.amyboyer.org> (19 September 2000).

2. Robert Scott, "Is Your Client a Stalker?" *P.I. Magazine*, Spring 2000, <http://www.crimetime.com/stalker.htm> (19 September 2000).

3. "Guarding Your Identity," *New York Times*, 7 September 2000 <http://www.nytimes.com/2000/09/07/opinion/07SAFI.html> (18 September 2000).

4. <http://www.amyboyer.org> (19 September 2000).

5. Minnesota attorney general's office, press release, 9 June 1999 <http://www.ag.state.mn.us/home/files/news/pr_usbank1_06091999.html> (21 September 2000).

6. Ibid.

7. "ACLU Sues Ohio School Board That Sold Students' Personal Information to the Bank," press release, 29 August 2000 <http://www.aclu.org/news/2000/n082900a.html> (20 September 2000).

8. Carrie Kirby, "Stolen Identity Poses Rising Crime Threat," *San Francisco Chronicle*, 11 February 2001, B1.

9. Ibid.

10. "Feeling Secure? Numerous Resources Can Help You Protect Your

Online Privacy," *Infoworld*, 8 September 2000 <http://www.infoworld.com/articles/op/xml/00/09/11/000911opbiggs.xml> (19 September 2000).

11. Sandeep Junnarkar, "Glitch Exposes Bank Customers' Account Information," *CNET News.com*, 15 September 2000 <http://news.cnet.com/news/0-1007-200-2784843.html?tag=st.ne.ron.lthd.ni> (21 September 2000).

12. Ibid.

13. Nando Times Staff, "New Zealand Man Confesses to High-tech Skirt Snooping," Reuters, 14 November 1997 <http://www.techserver.com/newsroom/ntn/info/111497/info12_10471_noframes.html> (21 September 2000).

14. Adam L. Penenberg, "The End of Privacy," *Forbes*, 29 November 1999 <http://www.forbes.com/forbes/99/1129/6413182a.htm> (21 September 2000).

15. John Bartlett, *Bartlett's Familiar Quotations*, Sixteenth Edition, Justin Kaplan, General Editor (Boston: Little, Brown, 1992), 398 n.1.

16. Neil Postman, *Technopoly: The Surrender of Culture to Technology* (New York: Vintage Books, 1992).

CHAPTER TWO

1. Philip Herrera, "What They Know About You," *Town & Country*, May 2000, 126.

2. Ibid.

3. Ibid.

4. Penenberg, "The End of Privacy."

5. Declan McCullagh, "Regulating Privacy: At What Cost?" *Wired*, 19 September 2000 <http://www.wired.com/news/politics/0,1283,38878,00.html> (22 September 2000).

6. Penenberg, "The End of Privacy."

7. "Dead Site? There Goes Privacy," *Wired News*, 30 June 2000 <http://www.wired.com/news/business/0,1367,37354,00.html> (22 September 2000).

8. Ibid.

9. Ibid.

10. "Consumer Groups Criticize Amazon's New Privacy Policy," *CNN.com*, 1 September 2000 <http://www.cnn.com/2000/US/09/01/amazon.privacy.ap> (23 September 2000).

11. "Privacy Groups Break Ties with Amazon," *CNN.com*, 14 September 2000 <http://www.cnn.com/2000/TECH/computing/09/14/amazon.privacy.ap/index.html> (22 September 2000).

12. Linda Rosencrance, "Update: More.Com Defends Its Privacy Policy in Wake of Lawsuit," *ComputerWorld*, 18 September 2000 <http://www.idg.net/ic_248903_1773_1-483.html> (22 September 2000).

13. Meta Group, "Commentary: Complex Privacy Issues Demand Enforcement," *CNET News.com*, 18 September 2000 <http://news.cnet.com/news/0-1007-200-2810663.html> (23 September 2000).

14. See <http://members.tripod.com/~cyberstalked> (18 November 2000).

15. "Cyberstalking," *MSNBC.com* <http://www.msnbc.com/news/456390.asp> (27 September 2000).

16. "Fired Yahoo! User Drops Suit Over Privacy Breach," *New York Times*, 4 September 2000 <http://chicagotribune.com/business/businessnews/article/0,2669,SAV-0009040018,FF.html> (22 September 2000).

17. Dick Kelsey, "Survey: Privacy Not High Priority for E-Businesses," *Newsbytes* <http://www.newsbytes.com/pubNews/00/154799.html> (20 September 2000).

18. In September 2000 a jury found that Wal-Mart had invaded the privacy of a former employee and sullied his reputation. Store officials, along with local police, had come to his home and seized four hundred items. Though Wal-Mart officials initially stated that the goods were theirs, in the trial they eventually conceded that all but thirty-seven of the items should be returned to the gentleman. See Michelle Bradford, "Wal-Mart Held Liable," *Arkansas Democrat-Gazette*, 7 September 2000, B6.

19. Snapshot, "Big Brother," *USA Today*, 23 June 2000 <http://www.usatoday.com/snapshot/life/lsnap169.htm> (28 February 2001).

20. The information in this Privacy Tip comes from a number of sources. See Karen L. Casser, "Employers, Employees, E-mail, and the Internet," *The Internet and Business: A Lawyer's Guide to the Emerging Legal Issues*, Joseph F. Ruh Jr., ed. (Fairfax, VA: Computer Law Association, 1996) <http://www.cla.org/RuhBook/chp6.htm#name> (28 February 2001); Eric S. Friebrun, Esq., "E-mail Privacy in the Workplace—To What Extent?" <http://www.cl.ais.net//lawmsf/articl9.htm> (28 February 2001); Laura Pincus Hartman, "The Rights and

Wrongs of Workplace Snooping" <http://www.depaul.edu/ethics/monitor.html> (28 February 2001); Jeff Mathias, "Workplace Privacy Rights," *Prairielaw.com* <http://prairielaw.com/articles/article.asp?channelId=20&articleId=1118> (28 February 2001); Barbara Kate Repa, "Computers and Email on the Job: They're Watching You," *Nolo Legal Encyclopedia* <http://www.nolo.com/encyclopedia/articles/emp/computers.html> (28 February 2001); Repa, "Telephones and Voicemail at Work: Can Your Employer Spy on You?" *Nolo Legal Encyclopedia* <http://www.nolo.com/encyclopedia/articles/emp/telephones.html> (28 February 2001); Jennifer Vogel, "The Walls Have Eyes," *PBS.org* <http://www.pbs.org/weblab/workingstiff/features/ionu.html> (28 February 2001); and "Workplace Privacy: Your Employer Knows More Than You Think," *Smart Computing*, March 2000 <http://www.smartcomputing.com/editorial/article.asp?article=articles/2000/s1103/22s03/22s03.asp> (28 February 2001).

21. "About.com Accidentally Releases Clients' Emails," *AZTechBiz.com*, 11 September 2000 <http://www.aztechbiz.com/news/20000911/144709> (22 September 2000).

22. Troy Wolverton, "IKEA Exposes Customer Information on Catalog Site," *CNET News.com*, 6 September 2000 <http://news.cnet.com/news/0-1007-200-2709867.html> (22 September 2000).

23. Linda Rosencrance, "Glitch at Amazon.com Exposes Clients' E-mail Addresses," *ComputerWorld*, 6 September 2000 <http://www.computerworld.com/cwi/story/frame/0,1213,NAV47-68-84-88-93_STO49648,00.html> (20 September 2000).

24. Ibid.

25. Troy Wolverton and Stefanie Olsen, "Eve.com Scrambles to Assess Security Breach," *CNET News.com*, 13 September 2000 <http://news.cnet.com/news/0-1007-200-2770505.html> (23 September 2000).

26. Troy Wolverton, "Netmarket Exposes Customer Order Data," *CNET News.com*, 10 May 1999 <http://news.cnet.com/news/0-1007-200-342300.html> (23 September 2000).

27. "Report Raises Questions Over Web Security" *CNN.com*, 14 September 2000 <http://www.cnn.com/2000/TECH/computing/09/14/britain.websecurity/index.html> (23 September 2000).

28. Todd Weiss, "Western Union.com Back Online After Theft of Credit-Card

Data," *ComputerWorld*, 14 September 2000 <http://www.computerworld.com/cwi/story/0,1199,NAV47-68-84-88-93_STO50212,00.html> (23 September 2000).

29. "FTC Wins $37.5 Million Judgment from X-Rated Web Site Operators," Federal Trade Commission, 7 September 2000 <http://www.ftc.gov/opa/2000/09/netfill.htm> (1 January 2000).

30. D. Ian Hopper, "Slammed with Scam: Website Owners Pay Millions for Bogus Charges," *ABC News.com*, 7 September 2000 <http://www.abcnews.go.com/sections/tech/DailyNews/webscam000907.html> (23 September 2000).

31. Jane Bryant Quinn, "How Do Telemarketers Learn So Much About You? Your Bank," *Daily Camera*, 26 July 1999 <http://boulderdailycamera.com/business/bp26quin.html> (23 September 2000).

32. Ibid.

33. Ibid.

34. See <http://www.dellvader.claritas.com/Express/freeinfo.wjsp> (14 October 2000).

CHAPTER THREE

1. Michelle Brown, "Identity Theft: How to Protect and Restore Your Good Name," Testimony before the Subcommittee on Technology, Terrorism, and Government Information of the Committee on the Judiciary, U.S. Senate, 12 July 2000 <http://www.senate.gov/~judiciary/7122000_mb.pdf> (1 January 2000).

2. Ibid.

3. Ibid.

4. "Don't Fall Prey to the Identity Thieves," *USA Today*, 12 September 2000 <http://www.usatoday.com/money/columns/block/0027.htm> (27 September 2000).

5. Associated Press, "Identity Theft on the Rise Despite New Laws," *USA Today*, 14 September 2000 <http://www.usatoday.com/news/ndswed07.htm> (14 September 2000).

6. In some cases, 411 operators will provide someone's current address—and for *free*—which is a good reason not to list your phone number.

7. See <http://www.digdirt.com/backgroundusa.htm> (26 September 2000).

8. See <http://www.nationwide-detective.com/search1.html> (23 September 2000).

9. See <http://www.ssntrace-search.com/background.html> (26 September 2000).

10. "Don't Fall Prey to the Identity Thieves," *USA Today.*

11. Brian Krebbs, "Financial Privacy Elusive in Wake of New Privacy Laws," *Newsbytes,* 13 September 2000 <http://www.newsbytes.com/pubNews/00/155149.html> (27 September 2000).

12. Mark Larabee, "Identity Crime Fought Face-to-Face," *Oregonian,* 21 September 2000 <http://www.oregonlive.com/news/oregonian/index.ssf?/news/oregonian/00/09/cu_51theft21.fram> (27 September 2000).

13. Associated Press, "Identity Theft on the Rise Despite New Laws."

14. Julia Angwin, "Credit Card Fraud Has Become a Nightmare for E-Merchants," *Wall Street Journal,* 19 September 2000 <http://www.msnbc.com/news/462835.asp?cp1=1> (27 September 2000).

15. See "Credit Card Loss Protection Offers: They're the Real Steal," *FTC Consumer Alert,* October 2000 <http://www.ftc.gov/bcp/conline/pubs/alerts/lossalrt.htm> (30 December 2000).

16. "Cyberstalking," *MSNBC.com* <http://www.msnbc.com/news/456390.asp> (27 September 2000).

17. Dan Goodin, "Cyberstalking Law Snags Alleged Violator," *CNET News.com,* 25 January 1999 <http://news.cnet.com/news/0-1005-200-337787.html?tag=st.ne.1002.srchres.ni> (27 September 2000).

18. Gina Edwards, "Marco Island Couple Sued for $10 Million in Internet Cyberstalking Harassment Suit," *Naples/Collier News,* 16 January 2000 <http://www.naplesnews.com/today/local/d387482a.htm> (27 September 2000).

19. Mike Brunker, " 'Cybersmeared': One Victim's Tale," *MSNBC.com* <http://www.msnbc.com/news/334729.asp> (27 September 2000).

20. Stefanie Olsen, " 'CueCat' Users' Information Let Out of the Bag," *CNET News.com,* 18 September 2000 <http://news.cnet.com/news/0-1007-200-2810594.html> (27 September 2000).

21. Bob Sullivan, " 'Netspionage' Costs Millions," *MSNBC.com,* 11 September 2000 <http://www.msnbc.com/news/457161.asp?cp1=1> (27 September 2000).

22. Autumn De Leon, "You've Got Hell," *Time,* 17 May 1999 <http://www.time.com/time/digital/magazine/articles/0,4753,51904,00.html> (27 September 2000).

23. "Cyberstalking," *MSNBC.com* <http://www.msnbc.com/news/456390.asp> (27 September 2000).

CHAPTER FOUR

1. "At Privacy Conference, Government Regulation Starts to Look Inevitable," *ComputerWorld*, 15 September 2000 <http://www.computer-world.com/cwi/story/0,1199,NAV47_STO50450,00.html> (28 September 2000).

2. See <http://frwebgate.access.gpo.gov/cgi-bin/get-cfr.cgi?TITLE=31&PART=103&SUBPART=B&TYPE=TEXT> (29 September 2000).

3. See <http://www.moneylaundering.com/SuspiciousActivity.htm> (29 September 2000).

4. Anthony Kimery, "Big Brother Wants to Look into Your Bank Account (Any Time It Pleases)," *Wired*, December 1993 <http://www.wired.com/wired/archive/1.06/big.brother.html?topic=&topic_set=> (29 September 2000)

5. Ibid.

6. Declan McCullagh, "Cash and the 'Carry Tax,' " *Wired News*, 27 October 1999 <http://www.wired.com/news/politics/0,1283,32121,00.html> (29 September 2000).

7. "New Director Seeks to Make Treasury Agency a 'Buzzword' in U.S. Law Enforcement Community, Reports *Money Laundering Alert*," press release, 28 June 1999 <http://www.moneylaundering.com/Pressjuly99.htm> (29 September 2000).

8. Declan McCullagh, "Feds: Digital Can Thwart Us," *Wired*, 22 September 2000 <http://www.wired.com/news/politics/0,1283,38955,00.html> (29 September 2000).

9. Patrick Poole, "Echelon: America's Secret Global Surveillance Network," 1999/2000 <http://fly.hiwaay.net/~pspoole/echelon.html> (29 September 2000).

10. See "Frequently Asked Questions About Echelon" from the ACLU's *Echelon Watch* Web site <http://www.aclu.org/echelonwatch/faq.html> (3 January 2000).

11. Ibid.

12. Ibid.

13. "Ex-snoop Confirms Echelon Network," *CBS News.com*, 1 March 2000 <http://cbsnews.com/now/story/0,1597,164651-412,00.shtml> (3 January 2000).

14. Suzanne Daley, "An Electronic Spy Scare Is Alarming Europe," *New York Times*, 24 February 2000 <http://www.nytimes.com/library/tech/00/02/biztech/articles/24spy.html> (3 January 2000).

15. Charles Trueheart, "Europeans Decry U.S. Electronic Intercepts," *Washington Post*, 24 February 2000 <http://www.washingtonpost.com/wp-dyn/articles/A24275-2000Feb23.html> (3 January 2000).

16. "France Accuses U.S. of Spying," *BBC News*, 23 February 2000 <http://news2.thls.bbc.co.uk/hi/english/world/newsid_654000/654210.stm> (3 January 2000).

17. Poole, "Echelon: America's Secret Global Surveillance Network."

18. Ibid.

19. Ibid.

20. Ibid.

21. Nick Wingfield, Ted Bridis, and Neil King Jr., "EarthLink Just Says No to FBI's Carnivore," *ZDNet News*, 14 July 2000 <http://www.zdnet.com/zdnn/stories/news/0,4586,2603945,00.html> (29 September 2000).

22. Associated Press, "EarthLink Dodges FBI's Carnivore," *USA Today*, 14 July 2000 <http://www.usatoday.com/life/cyber/tech/cti231.htm> (29 September 2000).

23. Associated Press, "FBI E-Mail Snooping Sparks Controversy," *USA Today*, 13 July 2000 <http://www.usatoday.com/life/cyber/tech/cti213.htm> (29 September 2000).

24. Declan McCullagh, "Carnivore Review Team Exposed!" *Wired News*, 27 September 2000 <http://www.wired.com/news/politics/0,1283,39102,00.html> (29 September 2000). *Wired* reported that the reviewers were known to "enjoy a close relationship to the Federal Government in general and to the Clinton Administration in particular."

25. See <http://cryptome.org/carnivore-mask.htm> (29 September 2000).

26. Ibid.

CHAPTER FIVE

1. Rory J. O'Connor, "Trading Net Privacy at E-Checkout," *ZDNet News*, 11 September 2000 <http://www.zdnet.com/intweek/stories/news/0,4164,2626162,00.html> (2 October 2000).

2. Ibid.

3. I've changed their names to protect their identities.

4. In the Bible, Jesus in fact offers wisdom on preparedness:

> For which one of you, when he wants to build a tower, does not first sit down and calculate the cost, to see if he has enough to complete it? Otherwise, when he has laid a foundation, and is not able to finish, all who observe it begin to ridicule him, saying, "This man began to build and was not able to finish." Or what king, when he sets out to meet another king in battle, will not first sit down and take counsel whether he is strong enough with ten thousand men to encounter the one coming against him with twenty thousand? Or else, while the other is still far away, he sends a delegation and asks terms of peace (Luke 14:28–32).

5. Kenneth W. Prewitt, Director, Bureau of the Census, Prepared Statement before the Subcommittee on the Census, U.S. House of Representatives, 5 May 2000 <http://www.house.gov/danmiller/census/testimony/5_5prewitt.html> (2 October 2000).

6. Ibid.

7. Bernstein, "Lives on File: The Erosion of Privacy."

CHAPTER SIX

1. Ted Leventhal, "GE Secretly 'Brought Good Names to Light,' " *Privacy Times*, 4 June 1999 <http://www.privacytimes.com/ge.htm> (10 October 2000).

2. Ibid.

3. Ibid.

4. Ibid.

5. Ibid.

6. "GE Investments Shareholders Miffed," *Indian Express Newspapers*, 13 June 1999 <http://expressindia.com/fe/daily/19990613/fex13032.html> (10 October 2000).

7. Ibid.

8. Leventhal, "GE Secretly 'Brought Good Names to Light.' "

9. "GE Investments Shareholders Miffed," *Indian Express Newspapers*.

10. John Bartlett, *Bartlett's Familiar Quotations*, Tenth Edition (1919). See <http://www.bartleby.com/100/620.5.html>.

11. According to privacy consultant J. J. Luna, in certain situations you won't be legally required to give your Social Security number. If you're certain that the organization won't check what you provide, you might, Luna says, consider providing a Social Security number other than your own. But you shouldn't simply transpose digits or make up any old number; that number will likely belong to a real person. Instead, you should consider a number that could not belong to someone else. Among the Social Security numbers that will never be assigned are: any number in which one of the three fields is all zeros; the ten Social Security numbers from 987-65-4320 to 987-65-4329, which are used in commercials; and the number 078-05-1120, which came with the sample Social Security card that many wallets used to feature.

12. See <http://www.cpsr.org/cpsr/privacy/ssn/SSN-History.html#protect> (27 February 2001). Used by permission.

13. You can download this from the United States Postal Service Web site at <http://new.usps.com/pdf/ps1583.pdf>. This document is in PDF format. You will need the Adobe Reader installed to read or print it. You can download Adobe Reader for free at <http://www.adobe.com>.

14. Ibid.

15. See <http://www.acl.fi/security/faq_md.htm> (10 October 2000).

16. See <http://emailaddresses.com/email_web.htm> (18 November 2000).

17. See <http://www.emailaddresses.com/guide_facts1.htm> (18 November 2000).

CHAPTER SEVEN

1. See <http://privacy.net/proxy>.

2. Fred McLain, "The Exploder Control Frequently Asked Questions," 7 February 1997 <http://www.halcyon.com/mclain/ActiveX/Exploder/FAQ.htm> (19 October 2000).

3. See <http://www.crak.com>.

4. You can read more about this product at <http://www.targus.com>.

5. Ibid.

6. Reuters, " 'Love' Bug Suspect Freed Pending More Evidence," *CNET News.com*, 9 May 2000 <http://news.cnet.com/news//0-1003-200-1843404.html> (13 October 2000).

7. Paul Festa, " 'I Love You' Virus Has 'Very Funny' New Name," *CNET News.com*, 4 May 2000 <http://news.cnet.com/news/0-1003-200-1815107.html> (13 October 2000).

8. Paul Festa and John Borland, "Experts Say 'Love' Spawns at Least 8 Mutations," *CNET News.com*, 5 May 2000 <http://news.cnet.com/news/0-1003-200-1817112.html> (13 October 2000).

9. Ibid.

10. See <http://vil.mcafee.com/dispVirus.asp?virus_k=10566&> (13 October 2000).

11. See <http://www.bo2k.com>.

12. See <http://www.cultdeadcow.com>.

13. "Surf Safely: Protect Your Messages," *CNET News.com* <http://www.cnet.com/internet/0-3761-7-2426167.html?tag=st.int.3761-7-2426162.txt.3761-7-2426167> (13 October 2000).

14. Ibid.

15. See <http://www.hushmail.com/what_is_hushmail.htm>. According to the site: "HushMail provides transparent key management. HushMail is the first Web-based e-mail service that exchanges the electronic keys necessary to encrypt and decrypt messages for Hush users automatically. Other services require that users manually exchange keys. With HushMail, you won't have to find a secure phone line, exchange long strings of numbers, or figure out how to download and upload messages from a 'secure' server. Hush users are free to exchange messages securely without the confusing, time consuming extra steps required by other secure messaging services."

16. See <http://www.compelson.com/pofi.htm>.

17. Actually, the Web site is <https://www.steganos.com>.

18. See <http://www.zonealarm.com/products.htm>.

19. See <http://www.guidancesoftware.com/encase/frame_encase.html>.

20. See <http://www.digitalintel.com/fred.htm>.

21. See <http://www.evidence-eliminator.com/main.shtml?>.

22. See <http://www.baxbex.com/cryptomite.html>.

23. See <http://www.gale-force.com/shredder95/indexa.html>.

CHAPTER EIGHT

1. Lucy Lazarony, "Privacy Paradise: Vermont and Alaska Keep Financial Information Under Wraps," *Bankrate.com*, 28 August 2000 <http://www.bankrate.com/brm/news/bank/20000828.asp> (16 October 2000).

2. Ibid.

3. Ibid.

4. Radio Shack seems to be the one exception to this rule, although I am sure there are others. Its employees have the annoying habit of asking for all kinds of personal information, even when you are making a cash purchase. This is a good way to test your resolve. Just refuse to give them the information. Or, if you don't want the hassle or are in a hurry, give them your secondary layer of ID as outlined in Chapter 6.

5. <http://www.nocards.org/faq/index.shtml> (14 October 2000).

6. See <www.nocards.org>. This list is used by permission.

7. See <http://www.travelersexpress.com/mo.htm>.

8. Dagan McDowell, "Is One-Stop Shopping for Financial Services Good for You?" 1 September 2000 <http://biz.yahoo.com/ts/000901/fund1_000901.html> (14 October 2000).

9. Ibid.

10. *Derbyshire v. United Builders Suppliers, Inc.*, 392 S.E.2d 37 (Ga. Ct. App. 1990). Morris, Manning & Martin, L.L.P., "Piercing the Veil of LLCs and LLPs," 5 August 1998 <http://www.mmmlaw.com/articles/memorandum.html> (18 October 2000). According to this memorandum:

> In Georgia, in order to succeed in piercing the veil of a corporate defendant, a plaintiff must show that "the stockholders' disregard of the corporate entity made it a mere instrumentality for the transaction of their own affairs; that there is such unity of interest and ownership that the separate personalities of the corporation and the owners no longer exist; and to adhere to the doctrine of the corporate entity would promote injustice or protect fraud." *Trans-American Communications, Inc. v. Nolle*, 214 S.E.2d 717, 719 (Ga. Ct. App. 1975). A plaintiff cannot reach the jury on the issue of piercing the corporate veil unless evidence exists "that the corporate arrangement was a sham, used to defeat justice, to perpetrate fraud or to evade

statutory, contractual or tort responsibility." *Derbyshire v. United Builders Suppliers, Inc.*, 392 S.E.2d 37 (Ga. Ct. App. 1990).

11. It should be noted that pure trusts have received a bad name recently. In some circles, people have attempted to use them for tax avoidance—or, from the government's perspective, tax evasion. The IRS has all but declared war on them. Therefore, I can recommend them only for privacy and asset protection.

12. Larry Sontag, *Privacy: It's None of Your Business* (Seattle: Peanut Butter Publishing, 1998), 163.

13. Arnold Cornez, *The Offshore Money Book: How to Move Assets Offshore for Privacy, Protection, and Tax Advantage* (New York: Contemporary Books, 1998), 1–2.

14. Ibid., 1.

15. Ibid., 30.

16. Ibid., 29–32.

17. Catherine Wilson, "IRS May See Credit Card Records," *Yahoo! News*, 30 October 2000 <http://dailynews.yahoo.com/h/ap/20001030/bs/credit_havens_1.html> (8 November 2000).

CHAPTER NINE

1. Harvey J. Platt, "The Living Trust: A Multipurpose Trust" <http://www.allworth.com/Articles/article29.htm> (20 October 2000).

2. IFC Trust Tutorial, Class One, Lesson 9 <http://www.cyberhighway.net/~mstarone/lesson9.htm> (20 October 2000).

3. The best way to do this, if at all possible, is to have the trust (or LLC or IBC or whatever you have chosen) purchase the house and set up utilities, phone, and so on, six to eight weeks *before* you leave your old home. That way, a private investigator won't be able to look at a list of phones that were connected the same month you left your old home in order to track down which one is yours.

4. "Protect Your Mail!" <http://www.acl.fi/security/maildrops.shtml> (10 October 2000).

CHAPTER TEN

1. Institute for Health Care Research, Georgetown University, "Health Privacy 101" <http://www.healthprivacy.org/info-url_nocat2302/info-url_nocat.htm> (28 February 2001).

2. Laura Beil and Charles Ornstein, "Patients' Data Not So Private," *Dallas Morning News*, 17 September 2000 <http://www.dallasnews.com/science/171774_privacy_17dis.html> (23 October 2000).

3. Ibid.

4. See, for example, Janlori Goldman and Zoe Hudson, "Exposed: A Health Privacy Primer for Consumers" (Washington, DC: Health Privacy Project, 1999) <http://www.healthprivacy.org/usr_doc/33806.pdf> (28 February 2001).

5. The MIB describes itself this way: "MIB, Inc. ('MIB') is a voluntary membership association of life insurance companies in the United States and Canada, with about 600 members and over 1000 locations. MIB is incorporated in Delaware as a non-stock, not-for-profit company. Our corporate headquarters and principal place of business is located in Westwood, Massachusetts, where we have about 180 employees. MIB also has an office in Toronto, Ontario, Canada. The Canadian office provides administrative support to our members and consumer information services to our consumers in Canada."

6. Frederick H. Fern, "Legal Implications of Electronic Transmission of Patients' Records in the Managed Care Pharmacy Industry," *Compensation & Benefits Management*, Winter 2000, 37.

7. Goldman and Hudson, "Exposed: A Health Privacy Primer for Consumers."

8. Ibid.

9. "Nelson Vows to Protect Privacy," *Tampa Tribune*, 7 September 2000 <http://tampatrib.com/FloridaMetro/MGIGBV6XTCC.html> (8 September 2000).

10. Ibid.

11. Gaucher's disease is, according to the National Institute of Neurological Disorders and Stroke, "a metabolic disorder in which harmful quantities of a fatty substance called glucocerebroside accumulate in the spleen, liver, lungs, bone marrow, and, in rare cases, the brain." See <http://www.ninds.nih.gov/health_and_medical/disorders/gauchers_doc.htm>.

12. Department of Labor, "Genetic Information and the Workplace," 20

January 1999 <http://www.dol.gov/dol/_sec/public/media/reports/ genetics.html> (26 October 2000).

13. EPIC, "Medical Record Privacy," 1 March 1999 <http://www.epic.org/ privacy/medical> (26 October 2000).

14. Electronic Frontier Foundation ACTION ALERT, "H. R. 10 'Confidentiality' Legislation Undermines Medical Privacy," 23 September 1999 <http://www.eff.org/pub/Privacy/Medical/19990922_hr10_alert.html> (26 October 2000).

15. Goldman and Hudson, "Exposed: A Health Privacy Primer for Consumers."

16. J. J. Luna, *How to Be Invisible: A Step-By-Step Guide to Protecting Your Assets, Your Identity, and Your Life* (New York: St. Martin's Press, 2000), 69.

17. Ibid.

CHAPTER ELEVEN

1. Joey Haws, "Seniors Told to Guard Privacy," *Standard-Examiner,* 1 September 2000 <http://www1.standard.net/stories/local/09-2000/FTP0044@local@01seniors@Ogden.asp> (25 October 2000).

2. Ibid.

3. Ibid.

4. Luna, *How to Be Invisible*, 69.

5. Ibid., 118.

6. "Fake ID—Dangers and Rip-offs" <http://www.ariza-research.com/new-id/fakeid.htm> (28 October 2000).

7. Luna, *How to Be Invisible*, 85.

8. According to Stan Pierchoski, founder of the Pro Se Litigant School of Law, a person can use an alias as long as it is not used to misrepresent, deceive, or defraud. Aliases can be used to do business, for instance; one can set up bank accounts called "d/b/a," or "doing business as."

CHAPTER TWELVE

1. Electronic Frontier Foundation <http://www.eff.org/pub/Privacy/ Cordless_Wireless/cordless_law.article> (30 October 2000).

2. D. Ian Hopper, "Surveillance Laws Targeted on Hill," *Yahoo! News,* 6

September 2000 <http://dailynews.yahoo.com/h/ap/20000906/pl/congress_privacy_1.html> (7 September 2000).

3. Ibid.

4. Ibid.

5. Will Knight, "British Angered Over Cell Phone Tracking," *ZDNet News*, 1 August 2000 <http://www.zdnet.com/zdnn/stories/news/0,4586,2610119,00.html> (30 October 2000).

6. Ibid.

7. Almar Latour, "Mobile Positioning: Track Your Friends," *ZDNet News*, 2 September 2000 <http://www.zdnet.com/zdnn/stories/news/0,4586,2623279,00.html> (30 October 2000).

8. Knight, "British Angered Over Cell Phone Tracking."

9. "Wireless Devices Could Be a Privacy Nightmare," *AltaVista.com*, 29 October 2000 <http://live.altavista.com/scripts/editorial.dll?ei=2293219&ern=y> (1 November 2000).

10. Ibid.

11. Joseph Farah, publisher of the popular WorldNetDaily.com, provided his readers a list of those words and symbols that might attract Echelon's attention. The list features approximately 1,500 items. See <http://www.worldnetdaily.com/news/article.asp?ARTICLE_ID=14840> (1 November 2000).

12. Sara Robinson, "Cell Phone Flaw Opens Security Hole," *ZDNet News*, 18 September 2000 <http://www.zdnet.com/zdnn/stories/news/0,4586,2628754,00.html?chkpt=zdhpnews01> (30 October 2000).

13. Ibid.

14. Sontag, *Privacy: It's None of Your Business*, 98.

15. Luna, *How to Be Invisible*, 97.

16. "Judge Rules GBI Agent Entitled to Damages in Phone Suit," Associated Press, 1 April 1999.

17. Luna, *How to Be Invisible*, 102–103.

18. See <http://web.mit.edu/network/pgpfone> (1 November 2000).

EPILOGUE

1. Michael Della Bitta, "Digital Angel: The New Eye in the Sky," 16 October 2000 <http://www.foxnews.com/vtech/101600/da.sml> (1 November 2000).

2. "Digital Angel Breakthrough Technology Goes Live!" press release, *Applied Digital Solutions*, 31 July 2000 <http://www.adsx.com/ADSX/CDA/News/news_index/0,1136,430,00.html> (1 November 2000).

3. Della Bitta, "Digital Angel."

4. Guy Gugliotta, "Bar Codes for the Body Make It to the Market: Biometrics May Alter Consumer Landscape," *Washington Post*, 21 June 1999, A1.

INDEX